Working in Multi-professional Contexts

Education at SAGE

SAGE is a leading international publisher of journals, books, and electronic media for academic, educational, and professional markets.

Our education publishing includes:

- accessible and comprehensive texts for aspiring education professionals and practitioners looking to further their careers through continuing professional development

- inspirational advice and guidance for the classroom

- authoritative state of the art reference from the leading authors in the field

Find out more at: **www.sagepub.co.uk/education**

Working in Multi-professional Contexts

A Practical Guide for Professionals in Children's Services

John M. Davis & Mary Smith

Los Angeles | London | New Delhi
Singapore | Washington DC

© John M. Davis and Mary Smith 2012

First published 2012

SAGE Publications Ltd
1 Oliver's Yard
55 City Road
London EC1Y 1SP

SAGE Publications Inc.
2455 Teller Road
Thousand Oaks, California 91320

SAGE Publications India Pvt Ltd
B 1/I 1 Mohan Cooperative Industrial Area
Mathura Road
New Delhi 110 044

SAGE Publications Asia-Pacific Pte Ltd
3 Church Street
#10-04 Samsung Hub
Singapore 049483

Library of Congress Control Number: 2011938955

British Library Cataloguing in Publication data
A catalogue record for this book is available from the British Library

ISBN 978-0-85702-172-4
ISBN 978-0-85702-173-1 (pbk)

Typeset by Kestrel Data, Exeter, Devon
Printed and bound by CPI Group (UK) Ltd, Croydon, CR0 4YY
Printed on paper from sustainable resources

MIX
Paper from responsible sources
FSC
www.fsc.org   FSC® C013604

Contents

List of abbreviations

CAF	Common Assessment Framework
CCUO	Coalition of Childhood Umbrella Organisations
CEDEFOP	European Centre for the Development of Vocational Training
CERI	Centre for Educational Research and Innovation
CREANOVA	Creative Learning for Innovation
CSPG	Children's Services Planning Group
DfE	Department for Education
DfES	Department for Education and Skills
DUMB	distorting, undermining, minister-inspired and blocking improvement
EACEA	Education, Audiovisual and Culture Executive Agency
ECM	Every Child Matters
EDEN	European Distance and E-Learning Network
EFQM	European Foundation for Quality Management
EPPE	Effective Provision of Pre-School Education
EQF	European Qualifications Framework
GIRFC	Getting It Right For Every Child
HNC	Higher National Certificate
HND	Higher National Diploma
IRD	Inter-agency Referral Discussion
ISO	International Standards Organisation
NAIRO	National Association of Independent Review Organisations

RADAR   Results, Approach, Deployment, Assessment and Review
RIPE   Research/evaluation, Ideological positions, Political
             disputes and Economic realities
SCQF   Scottish Credit and Qualifications Framework
SCRA   Scottish Children's Reporter Administration
SMART   Specific, Measurable, Accurate, Realistic and Timed
SSSC   Scottish Social Services Council
TPS   Toyoto Production System
UEA   University of East Anglia
UPIAS   Union of the Physically Impaired Against Segregation
WAG   Welsh Assembly Government

About the authors

Dr John M. Davis is a Senior Lecturer at Moray House School of Education, University of Edinburgh where he teaches and researches on childhood, inclusion, disability, and social justice. He is currently chair of the Scottish Social Services Council Childhood Practice Development Group.

Dr Mary Smith has considerable experience of planning and delivering integrated children's services. Her roles have included new community schools, community learning and development and integrated service management. She is currently Head of Children's Services for a Local Authority in Scotland and is an Associate Lecturer at Moray House School of Education, University of Edinburgh.

Acknowledgements

Mary Smith

Firstly I would like to thank all of the children and families I have been involved with during my career. They have inspired me to improve my own practice and to develop the practice of the professionals that I work with. I have been very privileged in my career to work with great colleagues in a very forward-thinking local authority who have supported me to develop my knowledge and skills. My authority funded me to carry out a Doctorate in Education at the University of Edinburgh and this led me to teach on the BA Childhood Practice Degree. This book has been inspired by that experience and the students whose thirst for knowledge led them to challenge our ideas in ways that gave us new insights. I would like to thank John Davis for all his support and encouragement over the years which led me to achieve things I would never have thought possible and I would like to thank Jude Bowen and her colleagues at Sage for their support and encouragement with this book. Finally and as always, my love and thanks go to my long-suffering family who have supported me through the years of study and who will never believe me when I say never again because who knows where the journey goes now?

John M. Davis

I would like to thank once again Jude Bowen and her colleagues not just for their help with this book but also for their support with two previous books *Research with Children and Young People* and *Integrated Children's Services*. It has indeed been a privilege to have had such a generous opportunity to put down my/our ideas in these books. I would also like to thank the anonymous reviewer who gave us extremely valuable feedback on the earlier version of this book. The book involves the idea that interactive and collective processes enable innovation and creativity. Such creative collaboration with my friend Mary Smith has led to this book which is built on many hours of discussions, joint teaching and shared analysis of our experiences in children and family services. There have been difficult times along the way but our sense of humour and a shared willingness to go that extra yard has got us through to the completion of this text. It is my hope that this text does justice to the people who have influenced it and in particular the children, families, students, colleagues and friends who gave us many ideas. I would finally also like to thank my family and friends who have given me so much support while we have been writing this book.

1

Introduction: themes, issues and conclusions

Chapter Overview

This introductory chapter briefly maps out for you the structure of the book and explains who the book is for and how it might be used. It talks you through the key themes, issues and conclusions of specific chapters and identifies how each chapter will discuss particular concepts, structures and relationships of multi-disciplinary working. Each chapter includes a combination of interrelated academic content, case studies, key definitions and practical activities. The connections between this content are discussed in this chapter in order to demonstrate to you the integrated nature of the text. The overall aim of the book is to act as a helpful framework for developing your practice and therefore this chapter explains the relevance of each chapter for you so that you can clearly grasp why the book raises a specific theme, discusses a particular argument and unpacks a certain issue.

The book, its concept, why it is needed and who it is for

Studies on multi-professional working have found that some professionals feel ill-prepared for integrated working and have a lack of knowledge/skills concerning the management and leadership of integrated multi-professional services (Davis and Hughes 2005). Policies in the area of children and family services have advocated a more joined-up outcomes-based approach to service delivery that has to be underpinned by more precise processes of referral, recording, information sharing, assessment, management, planning, delivery, monitoring and evaluation (Walker 2008). Over a number of years we have worked with undergraduate students, postgraduate students and professionals involved in continual professional development to help them to develop their knowledge, values, skills and practices concerning multi-professional working. This book brings together our understandings that have developed from this experience with the findings of research and evaluation projects that we have carried out in order to clarify how such changes can be introduced in multi-professional working.

When working with learners we noticed that, whatever their position (student, practitioner, manager), they experienced uncertainty regarding multi-professional processes. We realised there was a need for a book that informed students about the contexts they were about to work in, that encouraged existing practitioners to see themselves as leaders, that persuaded managers to consider how they could develop supportive and innovative processes in their organisations and examined how multi-professional learning could foster innovation and creativity (a key issue in Chapter 7).

We had particularly noticed when working with undergraduate students on the new part-time BA Childhood Practice in Scotland (e.g. early years managers, educational welfare officers, family support workers, residential care workers and out-of-school managers) that we were asking them to question the processes and practices of multi-professional working in a context where their line managers and colleagues were as confused as them about the implications of new integrated agendas in children and family services.

We realised that we needed a book that involved work place activities that could be used beyond the university classroom to help not just our students but also their colleagues to better understand the context of their work (this idea was substantiated by the findings of the CREANOVA project discussed in Chapter 7). For example, we developed problem and scenario-based learning resources that enabled different types of staff to sit and discuss specific cases.

These approaches were particularly useful when we carried out continual professional development in local authorities (with educational professionals, social workers, health visitors, health therapists, school nurses, mental health nurses, general practitioners, etc.). However, we were also struck by the hierarchical nature of multi-professional groups and came to the conclusion that we had to promote learning approaches that encouraged students to see themselves as leaders whatever their role/title and to work in less top-down ways (this issue is explored throughout the book but specifically in Chapters 4 and 5). In particular we noticed that when students evaluated their services/practices hierarchical ideas sometimes led them to utilise top-down approaches to evaluation that prevented them engaging with participatory approaches (this issue is returned to in Chapters 3 and 6). Similarly, when we worked with diverse groups of students on our masters courses (e.g. principle teachers and teachers of guidance/learning support, language support teachers, social workers, community educators, etc.) we realised they had different conceptual starting points from which to develop their approaches to joint multi-professional working.

Our experience suggested to us that there was a need for a book that could be utilised by students, practitioners and managers to help them clarify their tensions, contradictions and frustrations concerning issues of information sharing, joint assessment and decision-making that they encountered on a daily basis (issues raised in Chapter 2). Therefore this book has been written for students and existing professionals in health, education and social work services to actively use as part of academic qualifications (e.g. during placement, workplace learning or joint multi-professional units/modules), continual professional training courses (e.g. that seek to develop on-the-job knowledge about multi-professional working) and workplace team meetings (e.g. that are trying to plan strategies to enable better participatory working with service users). Our hope is that the book will act as a positive stimulus for the development of discussions, processes and practices that lead to greater and more integrated multi-professional services.

The structure of the book

This book employs a range of case studies to question issues of integrated multi-professional working. Each case study has been chosen because it enables us to question different concepts, structures and relationships of multi-professional working from within the process rather than from any specific professional subject area. Each of the case studies utilises our experience of working, researching and evaluating in multi-disciplinary settings to pose you questions about your practice and the practice of others in order that you can begin to analyse the concepts, structures and relationships that underpin your work.

Each chapter includes three activities which ask you to reflect on issues that have been discussed; however, the book does not specifically provide answers to the questions posed in each chapter's activities because we are very critical of rigid techniques – we want to avoid the potential for dogmatic acceptance of our ideas and believe that your answers will be different depending on the contexts within which you work. Therefore, we encourage you to avoid taking our ideas for granted, to be critical of our writing and to question our thoughts, preconceptions and positions.

Chapter 2   Multi-professional assessment, planning and delivery

It has been argued that there is conflicting evidence concerning the utility of tools of joint assessment, that too much focus has been put on child protection/regulatory process in children and family services and that workers do not have sufficient knowledge of early intervention approaches (Munroe 2011). It has been suggested that more emphasis needs to be placed on learning opportunities that develop practitioners knowledge and skills concerning multi-professional assessment and early intervention (Munroe 2011). This chapter seeks to increase your understanding of multi-professional assessment, planning and delivery by examining a case study of Dunlean local authority where a specific situation escalated into an acute child protection referral. (Note that Dunlean is a fictitious local authority we have constructed. However, its processes are drawn/amalgamated from actual evaluations we have carried out in a number of Scottish local authorities.)

The chapter asks you to consider the Dunlean example when analysing the difference between deficit and more contemporary strengths-based approaches to children, families and communities. It argues that strengths-based approaches require you to recognise the system in which the children and families live and require you to avoid working with children/parents in isolation from each other. It specifically encourages you to attempt to support service users in their communities, balance issues of autonomy, enable shared decision-making, question standardised approaches, engage with the politics of service delivery and ensure that service users experience trusting and flexible services.

The chapter frames the case study with a discussion of policies on assessment that have called for earlier intervention in families problems, promoted ideas concerning shared multi-professional assessment, advanced the notion of standardised record keeping across agencies and advocated the idea that a lead professional will be accountable. The chapter concludes by suggesting that you need to consider a complex interplay of conceptual, structural and relational issues when developing the practice of early intervention and that the shift to strengths-based approaches requires you to balance individual/shared judgement, build strong local relationships, have clearly defined procedures and have a committed approach to seeking out/sharing information in your work. It specifically concludes that in the case of Dunlean, more effort should have been put into developing at an earlier stage an understanding of the views of the children and adults involved. This issue of service user participation is revisited in Chapter 3.

Chapter 3   Participation and multi-professional working

Chapter 3 contains a case study of a one point multi-disciplinary children and family service in an English local government setting. The case study is included with the kind permission of Liam Cairns at Investing in Children. The chapter discusses the different definitions of participation that have emerged within Childhood Studies, considers different structures/spaces of participation and offers you advice on how you can enable children to more systematically collaborate with adults, professionals and communities in processes of decision-making. The chapter encourages you to recognise the resources that service users' possess, to utilise processes of participation to jointly establish outcomes, to balance the development of mechanisms of participation with more relational approaches and to create spaces to collaboratively analyse the diverse meanings of multi-professional service delivery.

The chapter connects different approaches to participation that are employed by Investing in Children such as agenda days, staff development programmes, collaborative membership schemes, information/research sharing, etc., to the need to enable service users to experience different types of outcomes including rights, local conflict resolution, stronger relationships, moral responses, recognition of injustice, social integration, social dynamism, the redistribution of resources and the removal of structural barriers such as transport and housing issues. The chapter demonstrates that participation processes need to be proactive and well resourced. It argues that the values of participation need to be embedded into organisational structures/cultures but it also points out that the first and simplest form of participation involves face-to-face discussion between professionals and service users.

You are encouraged to consider the relevance of Investing in Children's approach for your organisation, for example whether the approaches Investing in Children use to embed practice such as training, conceptual analysis, group membership and collaborative knowledge sharing have any value for you. You are also encouraged to consider what a culture of participation would look like in your organisation, to analyse whether people at different levels in your organisation have a commitment to social justice, diversity and thoughtfulness, and how you can support your organisation to practise the ideas of participation at different levels (e.g. with service users, practitioners, team leaders and senior management). The chapter concludes by encouraging you to adopt relational and collaborative approaches to multi-disciplinary service development that challenge subjective and hierarchical ideas concerning service users' abilities, view each participant as having their own type of expertise, balance formality/flexibility, question traditional organisational hierarchies, reject manipulative 'market choice' approaches to participation and confront deficit model approaches of exclusion. These ideas are picked up in Chapter 4 that investigates where the ideas that promote organisational hierarchy have come from.

Chapter 4   Traditional structures of multi-professional leadership and management

Chapter 4 draws from a case study of the development of a multi-disciplinary children and family service in 'Pentesk' Council in Scotland to demonstrate that hierarchical cultures in multi-professional services can foster:

- an unwillingness on the part of some professionals to move from outdated concepts of assessment

- the imposition of barriers to information sharing

- problems concerning recruitment and retention

- vested interests and traditions blocking change.

The chapter asks you to consider different concepts of and types of individual, group and professional leadership/management. It raises questions concerning issues of practice, policy, organisation and structure and contrasts technical rational ideas of leadership/ management with more relational approaches. The central aim of the chapter is to help you understand the restrictions of traditional command and control types of leadership and management (e.g. that they lead to blame cultures) and encourage you to begin to think about alternative relational approaches. It concludes (in keeping with Chapter 2) that you need to balance individual and collective ideas of leadership in multi-professional settings and by encouraging you to engage with relational approaches to leadership and organisational change, suggests that you can adopt a leadership role whatever your position in an organisation or community. This idea is returned to in Chapter 5 in relation to systemic approaches to service development.

Chapter 5   Contemporary approaches to multi-professional leadership and management

This chapter encourages you to promote change/development in your organisation that enables a range of people (children, parents, staff, etc.) to take leadership roles. It further develops the case study from Pentesk to analyse the different conceptual, structural and relational aspects of leadership and management and to encourage you and your colleagues to develop more reflexive, plural, responsive, integrated and multi-professional work spaces. It argues that over time relational approaches to service assessment and planning at Pentesk enabled coordinated multi-professional working to emerge in the integrated teams and forums (e.g. through joint training, trust-building processes, knowledge-sharing, joint problem-solving, etc.).

This chapter (in keeping with Seddon 2008 and Munroe 2011) also argues that we should employ ideas from systems theory to reduce waste in multi-professional services. It suggests that we should shift our focus from cuts to developing improved service outcomes and argues that waste in the system was reduced at Pentesk by developing and embedding flexible structures (common processes rather than identities) that enabled collective, diverse, reflexive, discursive and complex decision-making. It concludes that you can gain benefits from examining the complexity of local contexts; thinking about leadership as a variable thing; recognising that leadership can involve local consensus rather than top-down change and recognising the importance of dialogue, language and communication (Lawler and Bilson 2010).

Chapter 6   Multi-professional evaluation

This chapter further develops the notion of collective/collaborative reflexivity established in Chapter 5 and returns to the idea of participatory evaluation first discussed in Chapter 3. The chapter contrasts different structural approaches to research and evaluation with collective participatory and interrelational approaches. The chapter critically examines a case study of a Welsh multi-agency inclusion project evaluation carried out by an external consultant to consider what a more embedded approach to evaluation might look like. It critiques deficit type performance indicators (associated with total quality management) and contrasts them with outcomes developed through community dialogue. The chapter concludes by encouraging you to move beyond notions of performance and inspection to develop collaborative evaluations of services based on service users' experiences, participants' capacities and the idea that all partners in multi-professional services can locally contribute to the co-construction of collaborative knowledge and learning networks across multi-professional settings. The idea of collaborative learning networks is further explored in Chapter 7 which also revisits the idea from Chapter 5 that multi-professional working should involve collaborative innovation and creativity.

Chapter 7   Multi-professional learning and creativity

This chapter utilises findings from the Creanova Research Project (a major EU project funded under the Transversal Research element of the Lifelong Learning Programme European Commission Project No. 143725-LLP-1-2008-1-ES-KA1-KA1SCR that involved universities, regional governments and learning-design specialists). It analyses one of the CREANOVA case studies: an evaluation of a multi-professional mentoring course developed by the University of Edinburgh that was run in collaboration with the Coalition of Child Care Umbrella Organisations, the Scottish Social Services Council and the Scottish government.

The chapter encourages you to recognise that group processes can enable you to stimulate your individual creativity, that sharing enables you to draw on the creativity of others, that there are benefits to be gained from working with a range of people with different types of experience and that there are different structures, processes and relationships of dialogue in multi-professional settings. It suggests professionals that hide their feelings, errors or uncertainties (in an effort to keep up an apparently professional appearance) are actually unprofessional, that it is impossible as human beings for us to be perfect machines and therefore it is important within processes of professional development for you to examine your own preconceptions and those of your colleagues if we are to create collaborative and interrelational approaches to learning in multi-professional services that free up all participants (e.g. children, staff and managers) from processes of professional oppression.

The chapter connects ideas from the CREANOVA project concerning need, freedom, environment, interaction and design to discussions of professional learning to suggest that there is much to be gained from anti-hierarchical, interactive and collaborative multi-professional learning. It argues that innovation and creativity are embodied and embedded processes and that attempts to develop creative and innovative public services will benefit greatly from the understanding that creativity is not simply the domain of individual geniuses but is a capacity that we all possess that comes out most quickly when we interact with others in focused activities.

We hope that you enjoy the book as much as we have enjoyed writing it and actively use it with colleagues in your workplace. For, as Chapter 7 states, there is much to be gained from multi-professional collaboration and learning.

2

Multi-professional assessment, planning and delivery

Chapter Overview

This chapter considers a range of issues including: policies in children's services, the call for earlier intervention in family problems, the shift to shared processes of multi-professional assessment, the notion of standardised record-keeping and the emergence of lead professional accountability. The chapter analyses the case study of Dunlean (a Scottish local authority) in order to help you understand the connections between assessment policy, theory and practice. In considers the procedures at Dunlean in relation to hypothetical examples including an incident of domestic violence (involving Molly), the case of a girl (Frankie) who is exhibiting behavioural issues and the case of a girl (Jenny) receiving additional support at school. You are encouraged to adopt a strengths-based approach to assessment, information sharing and service delivery, and the chapter concludes by arguing that such approaches require you to build strong local relationships, have clearly defined but flexible procedures and have a committed approach to seeking out information in your work.

Dunlean Case Study

Throughout the chapter we refer to integrated assessment, planning and delivery procedures in children's services in a local authority we have given the pseudonym Dunlean. Dunlean is a constructed/fictitious local authority; however, its processes are drawn/amalgamated from actual evaluations we have carried out in a number of Scottish local authorities. The case study encourages you to question the roles and actions of the professionals involved and to consider the procedures for multi-professional assessment in Dunlean. These procedures include two defined roles: the 'named person' and the 'lead professional'. The 'named person' is a professional who comes from within universal services such as health/education and is allocated to every child (e.g. health visitors, early years nursery heads, primary/secondary school head teachers or devolved staff such as guidance teachers, therapeutic professionals, nursery practitioners and classroom teachers). The 'lead professional' is the professional who coordinates assessment, planning and delivery of services when a child has two or more agencies involved in their lives (Scottish Government 2010). In local services there can be lots of different people who consider themselves to be key workers (Davis and Hughes 2005; Davis 2011): those that are responsible for a child/communication with the family on a daily basis, link families to a range of services, carry out assessments, provide outreach work and coordinate service provision (Davis and Hughes 2005). However, in joint assessment frameworks the lead professional is the person who coordinates the provision and is the contact person for the child/family (Fitzgerald and Kay 2008).

In Dunlean this shift to recognising specific staff as having identified responsibilities within processes of assessment, planning and delivery was underpinned by staff training. Training was carried out on processes of gathering/analysing information, how to do holistic assessment (using the 'my world' triangle/resilience matrix), how to ensure delivery was outcome focused and how to complete chronologies of significant events in a child's life (Jack 1997; Daniel and Wassell 2002; Stradling et al. 2009). Reviews of such initiatives in Scotland found that many staff embraced new ways of working, developed stronger shared multi-agency thinking, became more confident in their approaches, began to share common understandings, co-constructed tools/processes/procedures and enabled greater involvement of children and family members in planning/review (Smith, M. 2009; Stradling et al. 2009; Smith and Davis 2010; Davis 2011).

Concepts of assessment

Frankie

Frankie aged 7 is behaving erratically in class, one minute upset and then becoming very angry and agitated. This behaviour presentation is unusual and the class teacher discusses Frankie with her head teacher at a pastoral care meeting in the school. Frankie's attendance at school has fallen lately and she has been late a number of times. The school had contacted mum who outlined that Frankie had a tummy bug or that they had slept in. It was agreed that because of the Easter break the behaviour might be due to Frankie needing time to settle back into the school routine. The school decide to monitor for two weeks to see if Frankie begins to settle and attendance improves.

Jenny

Jenny is 11 years old and is in specialist educational provision where she has regular reviews on a six-monthly basis. Jenny's mum is a single parent who supports Jenny and her younger sibling at a mainstream school. Jenny's behaviour has become more challenging of late and she is finding it very difficult in her peer group. Jenny has started soiling and wetting herself in class and the team are concerned about her presentation. She often arrives at school hungry and unkempt.

Jenny's mum arrived at the review meeting half an hour late looking a bit unkempt herself. The staff at the review meeting thought they smelt drink off mum's breath but put this down to mum perhaps having had a drink the night before. Staff discussed Jenny's soiling and wetting herself with mum and mum put this down to Jenny being bullied in class. The staff indicated that Jenny was supported in class and the playground but mum was adamant Jenny was being bullied.

The outcome of the review meeting was that Jenny would be offered more support in class and that the school nurse would address the issue of hygiene with Jenny. The school did not want to address the issue of both mum and Jenny appearing unkempt in case it made the relationship between mum and the school break down. Such situations are not unusual in settings where we work with children and families; however, this chapter will ask you to question the outcomes of the meetings that staff had with the parents of these pupils.

Families can experience services from a range of universal, targeted, daily, regular practitioners including 'regular specialists' on an outreach basis (e.g. peripatetic teachers/health visitors who may be attached to early years services), 'targeted specialists' (e.g. social workers, educational psychologists, speech and language therapists and other health-related specialists) who provide targeted, peripatetic, clinic-based or intensive/short-term support for care/learning/development and/or universal/regular practitioners (e.g. school teachers and some out-of-school/early years workers) (Davis and Hughes 2005). One of the problems identified with processes of joint assessment has been that this diverse range of professionals have had allegiances to different forms of assessment including individualised, ecological, multi-agency and politically nuanced holistic models (Davis 2011).

Individualised approaches

Individualised approaches have drawn from medical model and child development ideas to identify individual children's pathologies (Alderson 2000). In the case of Frankie she is assessed as being unsettled by a change in routine. This assessment reduces her life experience to a single psychological/individual cause. Similarly, Jenny was offered individual support but no effort was made to consider the behaviour of other children, to investigate bullying or to do a wider assessment. The children are judged against normative criteria of how they should individually behave (in a similar way that performance indicators have been used to judge adult service providers (Dahlberg et al. 2007)).

Such approaches to children's behaviour have often employed individual assessment scales and models (e.g. Goodman's, SDQ, Connors, Achenbach, etc.) that have tended to concentrate on specific behaviour (swinging on chairs, inattention, opposition to adult views) and privilege professional/adult views over those of children and young people. In particular they characterise children's behaviour as innate, subconscious and irrational (Davis 2011). In the past such concepts have led to child protection processes being criticised for downplaying children's abilities, failing to engage with the perspectives of children and families and constructing children/ families as incomplete, immature, irrational, inadequate, incapable and problematic (Moss et al. 2000; Smith and Davis 2010; Davis 2011).

Individualised objective/scientific approaches have been criticised by systems theorists in relation to local authority services that experience rationing (e.g. social care settings) because they have led to practitioners 'gaming' referrals (i.e. improving the criticality of a case in order to get it past the hurdles required to receive funding and support) (Seddon 2008). It has been argued that these particular approaches result in people wasting time on inappropriate assessments, form filling and shunting referrals instead of dealing with service users' issues at the first opportunity (Seddon 2008). Integrated services have been criticised when such approaches lead to people's life issues going unaddressed because staff are too keen to pass a case to another service in order to meet their target by closing 'their' file (Seddon 2008). Yet in the cases of Frankie and Jenny the problem was not one of inappropriate shunting of referrals. Rather, an opportunity was missed to understand their life issues from their own perspective and to contact other agencies. While Frankie's case seems straightforward, contemporary approaches to assessment recommend that we need to adopt shared approaches to judgement-making and involve a range of stakeholders' perspectives including the child, family, teachers, health and non-psychology/health professionals (Davis 2011; Munroe 2011). In this case Frankie's own views were not sought and a pattern had emerged that raised questions as to whether continued monitoring was appropriate. Frankie's named person (even at this stage) could have telephoned other professionals (within the area) to establish if they had any further information on her family or local context.

In relation to children's health services, it has been argued that individualised forms of assessment disempower children (Corker and Davis 2000, 2001). In the past such approaches in educational settings have tended to reify the deficits of disabled children, put forward the idea that their complex individual 'need' cannot be provided for in the mainstream system and resulted in requests for complex, segregated and specialist provision (Davis and Watson 2001). In Jenny's case, it is assumed that the provision of greater adult support will placate her mother and resolve the situation. Such approaches have been criticised in childhood studies for ignoring cultural diversity, failing to fully assess the social context of children's behaviour, under-representing children's capacities, ignoring the potential for children to possess formed identities, concentrating on children's inabilities rather than their abilities and using questionnaires that only take a few minutes to complete rather than properly investigating the issues in children's lives (Alderson 2000; Davis 2006).

The Getting It Right for Every Child (Scottish Executive 2005b) initiative had aimed to address such criticisms by ensuring that children received timely and appropriate interventions. It was similar to the Every Child Matters initiative in England that aimed to promote service, culture and practice change. Both approaches aimed to stimulate workforce reform, improve outcomes for children/families and promote more integrated approaches (e.g. improved information sharing).

The case examples raise questions for you as professionals as to how you can decide what an appropriate approach to assessment is. It has been argued that workers in multi-professional children and family services need to be able to exercise more judgement within processes of collective decision-making (Munroe 2011). For example, it is appropriate for a professional within a school to exercise their judgement; however, they need to ensure that they have carried out an appropriate assessment that includes the views of the child, family and other colleagues that work with the child. A key question in both cases would be, 'do the pupils have other siblings in other schools?' It may be that new information can be gathered by talking to siblings or the professionals who work with those siblings.

We encourage you to engage with and develop processes that involve the named person (or delegate) phoning colleagues within services, integrated teams or specialist services to ask if they have information pertinent to, have previously carried out an assessment of or are currently providing a service to a specific child/family. In this example, the specialist educational professionals in Jenny's case failed to see the mother's drinking as a possible sign and overlooked the potential that Jenny's mother may have been known to health services. Similarly, they appeared to ignore other potential signs relating to Jenny's appearance, hunger and hygiene. They did not appear to see themselves as part of a wider system.

Ecological assessment

Ecological models are based on the work of Bronfenbrenner (1989) that considered the social context of childhood. Such approaches have encouraged practitioners to adopt 'child-centred' perspectives and examine the social relationships around the child's life (e.g. family, school neighbourhood, etc.). They are similar to social capital ideas (that children derive educational and social skills, values and knowledge from their families and communities and therefore need services to address issues such as poor housing, lack of financial resources and gaps in community/peer/social support), holistic pedagogy perspectives (that services should be interested in the whole child mind, body emotions, etc.) and social model perspectives in disability studies that define disability as the barriers that disabled people encounter in their lives created by societal structures/attitudes (including inaccessible buildings, negative stereotypes about disabled people's inabilities, intransigent welfare rules) rather than by their medical impairments (Morrow 1999, 2000; Cohen et al. 2004; Dolan 2008; Davis 2011; UPIAS 1976). Such perspectives underpinned the development of the Additional Support for Learning (Scotland) Act 2004 which stated:

> A child or young person has additional support needs for the purposes of this Act where, for whatever reason, the child or young person is, or is likely to be, unable without the provision of additional support to benefit from school education provided or to be provided for the child or young person.
>
> (ASL Act 2004)

This legislation shifted the focus from assessment of specific individual medical impairments to issues that prevented learning that included:

- medical impairments

- being particularly talented

- parents abusing substances

- emotional issues

- bullying

- having language issues

- parents' mental health issues

- social/housing issues

- bereavement

- being looked after

- truanting

- being a young carer.

In particular this Act required education professionals in Scotland to carry out inter-agency assessments, take account of the views of children and parents and to develop coordinated support plans when more than one agency was involved.

Such approaches have enabled practitioners to become more 'client focused', view children as agents and include children in decision-making processes (Leathard 2003b; Rixon 2008b). For example, in the cases of Frankie and Jenny a discussion of their barriers to learning may have revealed a range of issues in their life worlds. A simple conversation with either Jenny or Frankie regarding the ecology of their life worlds would have found out that they were in fact siblings. It would then have been easy for the respective school heads to contact each other and discuss the cases.

It may be that the failure to carry out such a conversation related to political or cultural considerations concerning adult or professional power. While ecological approaches to integrated service assessment have been welcomed, they have also been criticised for not always dealing with the politics of children's services or challenging the assumption that adults know what is the best intervention for children (Davis 2007; Smith and Davis 2010; Davis 2011). Indeed, the professional's reticence to delve deeper into Frankie and Jenny's lives may have related to their difficulties with engaging with parents/children from culturally different/more impoverished communities, perceiving disabled children to be agents or understanding issues in their school beyond those concerning everyday curriculum delivery.

It should be noted that we are not trying to label professionals. There could also be systemic reasons for people not acting sooner such as problems with staff resources, issues with forthcoming inspections, lack of support from leaders/managers in the local authority and pressures from performance indicators. (Indeed performance targets can often be put before service user requirements as a method of worker survival (Seddon 2008; Munroe 2011).) Our view is that it is important that you apply the notion of ecology to all the individuals in the process and not simply the child. Indeed, this leads us to criticise the onion diagrams that are employed to explain ecological concepts of integrated assessment on the grounds that they place too much focus on the individual child (which is usually a big figure at the centre of the diagram) and not enough on the life conditions and capacities of the parents, professionals and community in the wider circles.

In our example the children were not properly consulted, solutions were rushed or delayed, decisions were only made by adults and (in the case of Jenny) responses were limited to simply more adult intervention. In any given situation you should explore the power relations within different service settings in order to better understand both the issues that underpin assessment/referral and to ensure that any solution is built on knowledge of the complexity of the situation that service users and providers find themselves in. Writing in other countries has analysed the power relations of integrated services and encouraged us to move away from approaches that impose eurocentric/culturally prejudiced notions on processes of assessment, exclude families from the assessment process, deny local choice/decision-making and ignore the potential for family/community self-help (Ball and Sones 2004; Moore et al. 2005; Davis 2011).

Inter-agency multi-professional approaches have sought to enable greater dialogue between parents, children and service providers. They have aimed to ensure that one professional perspective does not dominate service provision and that, by providing more thoughtful, flexible and complex service provision, waste is reduced in the system (in this case resources were wasted on the provision of inappropriate additional support for Jenny and initial meetings that led nowhere). Had both heads liaised and had discussions, the children's difficult life circumstances may have emerged and the heads could have asked their mother's permission to discuss their cases with other services. Such approaches require engagement from families (that is not always forthcoming) and for professionals to consider how their own fears, values and prejudice may impact on their work.

Politically nuanced holistic models

Politically nuanced holistic models have challenged the assumption that the professional is the totalising expert on any situation. These approaches have argued that children, peer group, families, communities, practitioners, leaders and managers all have different forms of expertise. They have utilised Bronfenbrenner's (1989) holistic approach but also connected it to more complex ideas concerning minimum intervention, service users' strengths, rights, social justice, redistribution, anti-discrimination, community collaboration and self-empowerment (Dolan 2006, 2008; Broadhead et al. 2008; Smith and Davis 2010).

It is possible to differentiate between those community-based approaches that are local, those that aim to build relationships, those that involve service outreach from a specific location, those that connect families to broader services/support systems and those that more specifically provide an identified context for planning, targeting of intervention and action (Chaskin 2006). In our example there appeared to be social distance between professionals in universal services such as education and health and the actual reality of the community within which Frankie and Jenny lived. For example, the educational professionals had the meeting concerning the children's 'problems' in their own location as they were perceived to relate to individual issues. A home visit might have brought out a different perspective on the contexts within which the children lived.

Contemporary approaches have encouraged you to be clear when trying to support service users' resilience and have proposed a set of approaches that can be effective when used together (e.g. those that reduce risk, stop negative chain reactions, promote self-empowerment/ esteem/efficacy, enable compensatory experiences, open up positive opportunities and analyse/promote understanding of negative experiences (Dolan 2006, 2008)). They have suggested that family support work should be built on values/processes (sometimes referred to as social support theory) that involve:

- partnership working with children, families, professionals and communities

- a requirements-led approach that strives for minimum intervention

- clear focus on the wishes feelings, safety and well-being of children

- a strengths-based/resilience perspective and strengthened informal networks

- accessibility and flexibility incorporating both child protection and out-of-home care

- self-referral and multi-access referral paths

- service users and frontline providers collaborating in planning, delivery and evaluation

- the promotion of social inclusion and addressing of issues of ethnicity, disability and rural/urban communities

- outcome-based evaluation that supports quality services based on best practice.

(Dolan et al. 2006: 13)

These approaches have highlighted the requirement for strong partnerships between children/professionals/families, clear agreements concerning joint assessment and intensive dialogue concerning the most appropriate solutions (Smith 2007). There has been a tradition of non-judgemental approaches to children in Scotland, for example the judicial system relating to children is traditionally based on 'needs not deeds' (Tisdall 1995). Hence, a child who has committed an offence will experience a similar judicial process to a child who has experienced abuse/neglect: the views of the child will be taken into account and they will be present during hearings.

In the cases of Frankie and Jenny this sort of participatory approach was not followed. They should have been consulted more quickly and asked to identify if there were errors in the adult professionals' conclusions. An opportunity was lost to open up discussion between the children and a range of professionals about identification, assessment and solutions. The opportunity was lost to carry out a joint assessment process that could sensitively work through the parent's and professionals' conflicting views concerning Frankie and Jenny's life issues. Professionals did not see the cases as potentially involving child protection issues, nor did they consider that the children required additional support beyond what could be offered in their respective schools. That is, there was professional concern but not dialogue.

In Dunlean local authority it was important for those receiving referrals to work out what an appropriate referral was. In particular there were some staff who held rigid deficit perspectives that constructed children and families as abnormal, deficient, weak, vulnerable, incomplete, immature, irrational, inadequate, incapable and problematic (Moss et al. 2000; Smith and Davis 2010; Davis 2011). These staff would not have been happy to have these cases referred to them as they only perceived themselves to work with acute cases concerning child protection, care and disability. They could be contrasted with those who held contemporary ideas (e.g. family support workers who recognised the diverse/complex nature of children's and parents' lives and were more aware of national well-being indicators (Smith and

Davis 2010; Davis 2011)). That is, there was a distinction between staff who understood politically nuanced integrated multi-professional working and those who did not.

 Activity

These examples demonstrate that the process of exercising professional judgement can be difficult. In particular, there are tensions between legislation/guidance, child protection procedures and joint assessment (Munroe 2011). Do you understand the different approaches that are used in your local area? Are you clear what your responsibility is, which professionals act as the named person or the lead professional and how to raise concerns? Are you clear about the different concepts that underpin assessment and the difference between individual, holistic and politically nuanced approaches? Can you compare our cases to examples in your own work? Can you discuss any concerns that you have about referring cases/sharing information with your colleagues? In particular, disabled children have been found to have been missed out in child protection processes (Stalker and McArthur 2010). Can you look on the Internet for examples of reports that give recommendations on how to ensure child protection procedures for disabled children are appropriate?

Structures of assessment

Molly

Molly attended her GP because she had undertaken a home pregnancy test and discovered she was pregnant. The GP discussed the pregnancy with Molly who was surprised by the pregnancy but delighted. Molly has two other children of 7 and 11 to her previous partner who she left due to domestic violence three years ago. Molly informed the GP that her current partner was also delighted and that they get on very well. The GP confirmed that Molly was around 12 weeks pregnant and referred her to the hospital for a scan. The GP informed the midwifery service of the pregnancy and alerted them to Molly's previous experience of domestic violence. Molly was monitored by the midwifery service and did not see her GP again until later in the pregnancy. At 24 weeks pregnant the midwife received a report from the police that Molly has been the victim of domestic violence the previous weekend. Although Molly did not want to press charges the referral was sent for information to both social work and the midwife.

The midwife received a telephone call from the duty social worker to discuss the police report. The referral stated that Molly's partner was drunk, there had been an argument and he had fallen over the glass coffee table causing broken glass to be strewn over the floor.

The social worker spoke to Molly on the telephone who stated that no one was injured and that this was the first incident within this relationship. The midwife advised the social worker that she had seen Molly that morning and everything was fine. Molly did not discuss the incident but indicated to the midwife that things were great and that the family was looking forward to the birth of the baby.

The social worker and midwife made the decision that they would take no further action at this point due to the fact that there had been no domestic violence incidents in the last three years and that Molly herself did not want to press charges. It was agreed that the midwife would continue to monitor Molly and report any concerns to the social worker.

Structures of joint assessment were developed as a response to a series of child protection enquiries, the perception that there had been a 'catastrophic failure' in welfare services and the view that we needed to move beyond the traditional child protection and single-service 'ownership' approaches of children and family services (Carpenter 1997; Leathard 1997; Millar 2006). Policy documents in the different jurisdictions/countries that make up the United Kingdom adopted an integrated and multi-professional language (including Every Child Matters (England), the 10-year Strategy for Children and Young People (Northern Ireland), Getting It Right for Every Child (Scotland) and Core Aims for Children and Young People (Wales)). Such documents promoted flexibility, diversity and inclusion; aimed to address issues of conflict; were concerned with issues that arose during service transition; called for greater information sharing; and aimed to address/improve issues related to education/learning, community development, environmental sustainability and economic well being (Davis 2011). They also called for coordinated planning and delivery at regional and local levels, promoted the concept of children's plans, highlighted the need to connect to local community processes and called for greater participation of children, young people and families (Smith 2009). In particular, policies in this area advocate a more joined-up outcomes-based approach that is to be underpinned by precise referral, recording, information-sharing, assessment, management, planning, delivery, monitoring and evaluation (Walker 2008; Munroe 2011).

The Common Assessment Framework (CAF) in England and Wales (relating to Every Child Matters) and the Integrated Assessment Framework in Scotland (relating to Getting It Right for Every Child) built on earlier attempts to move away from narrow child protection-focused approaches towards proactive approaches that intervene at an earlier stage (Jack 2006; Foley 2008; Jones and Leverett 2008; Walker 2008; Davis 2011; Munroe 2011). Joint, integrated and earlier assessment was advocated as a way of promoting multi-agency working when children and families experienced multiple issues such as drug abuse, alcohol abuse, anti-social behaviour, attendance issues, mental health concerns, welfare issues, etc. Joint assessment has been replicated and adopted in over 15 countries worldwide (Léveillé and Chamberland 2010).

The Common Assessment Framework was a standardised approach to assessing the needs of children and families. It aimed to encourage common understandings among professionals, parents and children. Similarly, the Integrated Assessment Framework sought to be a foundation for identifying concerns, assessing needs/risks and sharing language/understanding (Scottish Government 2010). Key components of both approaches included a central policy framework (ECM/GIRFEC), early identification, joint assessment, multi-agency working, training, standardised paperwork, named person, lead professional and three levels of provision (universal, targeted, complex). Joint assessment was intended to be a thoughtful process that acted as the basis for early intervention before problems could grow (Jones and Leverett 2008).

In Scotland the purpose of the Integrated Assessment Framework was to ensure that there was:

• holistic assessment of children's needs

- a reduction in the number of children being referred to the children's reporter (the Scottish Children's Reporter Administration (SCRA) is the statutory process of referral/decision-making on issues of care, welfare and youth justice)

- better integrated planning and a greater emphasis on engaging young people in the planning process

- greater emphasis on helping young people to take ownership of assessment, planning and delivery

- improved transition from care to adult life

- increased documentation of and recording of evidence for decision-making

- specific identification/clarification of the intended outcomes and evidence of progress in the children's plan.

(Stradling et al. 2009)

The Integrated Assessment Framework was established to ensure that the process of referral began when a concern was reported by member of the family, the general public or, more usually, a professional (e.g. the police). In particular, it was argued that adult services (e.g. GPs, community nurses) and services such as the police have a crucial role to play in recognising signs of neglect and abuse and triggering the need for multi-professional discussions and assessments (Munroe 2011).

In this case study professionals in Dunlean who had clear child protection concerns were expected to instigate an inter-agency referral discussion (IRD). This was to be quickly undertaken between health, police and social work to establish what/if any information was held and to discuss the level of concern. The inter-agency referral discussion was also expected to establish which agency/professional would lead an assessment. From this process (which is expected to happen in one day) the following decisions would be made:

- no further action

- a single agency response (e.g. social work, family support or health provision)

- referral to the reporter (e.g. where statutory provision such as a supervision requirement may be discussed)

- a multi-agency child protection response (e.g. where there is an initial child protection case conference)

- referral to multi-agency forum/discussion (e.g. where services are jointly coordinated).

Whatever the outcome of this process (with the exception of no further action), all children involved in these processes were expected to have their cases reviewed regularly in accordance with national legislative or policy requirements. This process was also to be carried out for unborn children.

In Molly's case there was no failure to exchange information. However, there was a lack of sharing of previous case history and no risk assessment was carried out for the unborn child or the siblings. The health visitor and the social worker accepted Molly's story and did not investigate further (agreeing to monitor the situation). This case is similar to that of Frankie in that the situation was to be monitored but it is more serious as there were more obvious issues that could have been spotted. These professionals could have instigated an inter-agency referral discussion due to their concerns.

Concepts of risk management have focused on preventing individual, collective or organisational failure. Such approaches have required individuals in organisations to assess, identify and rate the likelihood of risk by analysing their work environment, auditing case files (or other records), understanding incidents, examining complaints/compliments and establishing fault (Dickson 1995; McIver 2002; Simmons 2007; Lawler and Bilson 2010). Risk assessment processes have also required the identification of risk control/management factors (e.g. leadership, training, transfer of resources, structures of accountability, lines of supervision and reporting processes) (Dickson 1995; McIver 2002; Simmons 2007; Lawler and Bilson 2010). Risk assessment approaches have been perceived to be valuable as they have helped to shift the focus from crisis intervention (when things have reached a dramatic point too late in the process) and post-delivery/incident performance audit (when things have actually happened) to enable early intervention and preventative work (Glenny and Roaf 2008).

However, risk management processes have also been criticised as being too rigid, ignoring the complexities of services, trying to iron out all contradictions, assuming that increased proceduralisation is the solution and ignoring the possibility of developing complex responses to difficult situations (Simmons 2007; Lawler and Bilson 2010; Munroe 2011). Such critiques have shifted the emphasis from managing out risk to managing with uncertainty, suggesting that every case will have some ambiguous aspects and that the skill of the professional is to work with, plan for and accommodate different risks.

In the case of Molly the workers failed to instigate any process related to risk. Similarly, Frankie and Jenny were dealt with within their schools. Had a multi-agency referral discussion taken place concerning either Frankie or Jenny their connection would have become apparent, a lead professional would have been appointed, different services (including psychologists and therapists) would have helped write their service plans, their extended family could have been involved and appropriate support could have been put in place.

 Activity

Policies change with time and the implementation of policies can be problematic. However, the Scottish government introduced a number of documents that explained how Getting It Right for Every Child should be introduced. If you do not work in Scotland are you aware of such documents in your country? Can you discuss their utility with your colleagues? In Scotland, processes of assessment were supposed to lead to provision that ensured children experienced improved outcomes that related to national well-being indicators. Are you aware of what these are? If you use them have you asked children what they think about them? Are you sure that the outcomes are what children want/require?

Are you aware of assessment tools such as the well-being outcomes, the 'my world' triangle and the resilience matrix? Can you look for examples of them on the Internet? Can you see any gaps in these tools? Can you discuss these tools with colleagues and children you work with to see if they could be improved?

Relationships of assessment

Molly's house

Police are called to a house where a woman and her children are reported by a neighbour to be in a distressed state. When the police arrive the woman and her two children aged 7 and 11 are clearly distressed, huddled together and crying. The woman has clear bruising to her face and arms. The police note that the mother of the children smelled of drink, was slurring her words and there were empty bottles of beer/vodka strewn about the living room.

The woman claimed that her partner had been drinking all day and had become violent because the children had been fighting each other. Her partner had left the home and had gone to the pub.

On further investigation the police found that there was no food in the home, no heating or hot water and the house was filthy with the smell of faeces and urine. The children also only had one shared bed and this was sodden with wet and soiled sheets. The children (Frankie and Jenny) advised the police that their mum (Molly) and her partner (called 'Uncle Derrick') were always arguing, drinking and fighting.

The police called social work services as the conditions were so bad in the house that the children could not be left in the home with Molly. Molly confirmed that she was 24 weeks pregnant so they also called an ambulance to take her to hospital for a check-up.

The social worker allocated to the children immediately started gathering information from school, police, health and social work records so that they could then decide on the action to be taken.

Working out who should do assessments and issues with lead practitioners

Integrated services require strong relationships to be built with both parents and children but this process can be problematic if, for example, too many assumptions are made about parents' capacities to share information and enter into dialogue (Leathard 2003b; Foley 2008; Glenny and Roaf 2008; Jones and Leverett 2008). In the case of

Dunlean assumptions were made and situations were monitored when professionals should have acted. Most importantly, it took too long for the different agencies to connect with each other and therefore the fuller picture emerged too slowly. Of particular concern was the fact that the social worker and midwife at an early stage accepted Molly's explanations without gathering further information. They could/should have been more proactive about assessing the risk to the adults, children and unborn child.

This case demonstrates the need to connect information held in adult and children's services (Munroe 2011). In particular, an examination of information held on Derrick would have revealed issues of depression, instances of previous domestic violence to other partners and alcoholism. This case also encourages us to see adults' and children's worlds as connected and to recognise the importance of working with children at the same time as parents and peer groups (Dolan and McGrath 2006).

Children and young people who have been asked about service structures have suggested that they should be underpinned by the building of strong relationships (Davis 2011). They have suggested that services should enable them to avoid being shunted between providers, to be able to experience local services that are flexible to their needs (e.g. drop-in services) and to have easier/earlier access to people they can trust (Glenny and Roaf 2008; Davis 2011; Munroe 2011). They have also suggested that flexible integrated services should involve service providers creating strong collaborative relationships with their parents/relatives (Glenny and Roaf 2008; Davis 2011). There is much to be gained from processes that build flexible integrated relationships because they can ensure that resources are not wasted, that services take account of the life contexts of service users and that services take into account the capacity of children, parents, family members, professionals, community members and voluntary organisations to deliver positive outcomes (Davis 2007; Dolan 2008). However, in the Dunlean example, opportunities were missed to instigate an inter-agency referral discussion that would have led to greater multi-professional communication and an integrated assessment. Professionals failed to follow or were unaware of procedures that might have enabled the full picture to be established, for clear dialogue to emerge and for relationships to be built much earlier on an open and appreciative basis.

It is our perspective that professionals should be encouraged to exercise judgement, that we should avoid deficit approaches and that we should avoid processes of blame that may alienate children, parents and professionals. However, we have concerns when notions of flexibility lead to lassez-faire approaches, when formal processes are completely ignored and when professionals do not make the judicial/policy context of their work clear to children and families. That is, flexible approaches to assessment have to consider a tension involving the autonomy/surveillance of the child, family and worker but they do not require procedures to completely disappear. They have to balance the need for local decision-making with the need to follow frameworks/procedures. It is important for professionals to explain local/national procedures to children and families to ensure they understand the potential consequences that will occur if, for example, situations do not improve.

Similarly, it is important for professionals to be clear with colleagues about how they exercise individual and collective judgement, to jointly establish their expectations regarding procedures and collaboratively to examine the relational issues that can cause problems in integrated assessment. Research has shown us that relationships of multi-professional assessment can be problematic if:

- questions arise concerning role clarification, use of scarce resources and willingness to undertake more mundane tasks (Rowe 2005)

- agencies that are, for example, not the lead agency are reluctant to share information (Billingham and Barnes 2009)

- statutory services and specific professionals in key positions find it difficult to accept new ways of working (Fox 2005)

- local politics and vested interests result in agencies failing to fully support new initiatives (Smith and Davis 2010)

- practitioners vie for position, have no defined case load, see very few children/families and make a very small amount of home visits (Aubrey 2010)

- practitioners (e.g. social workers and educational psychologists) only provide general support outside of statutory processes (e.g. those related to children at risk, in care or experiencing disability) (Aubrey 2010).

Contemporary reports into issues of assessment have highlighted problems where professionals are so tied up with the management of procedures and performance indicators they no longer work with children and families on a face-to-face basis (Munroe 2011). Key failures in Dunlean involved a lack of information-sharing between professionals, insufficient home visits, disengagement with new ways of working, confusion concerning whose role it was to instigate an IRD and inadequate involvement of the children.

Children and young people turn to a range of people for help and advice, for example doctors, friends, teachers, work colleagues, help lines and advice centres (Davis 2011). Without integrated information sharing it is unlikely that one professional can gather sufficient information to build the full picture, particularly if the child is too scared or loyal to divulge their experience. Information was not gathered about Frankie, Jenny, Molly and Derrick because the professionals involved did not perceive their role as being located within a wider strengths-based context that would have required them to consider the holistic needs of this family and the possibility that support could have been provided to improve their living conditions by relatives, local organisations and other community members.

Information sharing

The most important aspect of multi-professional assessment is information. Information should be gathered in a systematic/precise way, should be up-to-date/accurate, should be kept within the requirements of data protection legislation concerning the display and sharing of information (e.g. not leaving information on a desk or sharing it only with people who have a need to know) and should not be shared without the reason for sharing being recorded (Walker 2008). Some professionals have argued that information/data-keeping is a burden on their work (Munroe 2011). However, we agree with those who suggest that the key issue is whether information enables you to understand the effectiveness of your work in terms of improved outcomes for children and families. Without clear information on service users' perspectives/requirements and a clear understanding of what the lines of communication are scarce public resources can be wasted (Seddon 2008).

In terms of cooperation, it has been suggested that information-sharing can be difficult as software systems may not be able to cope with change and individual agency records, information systems and retrieval processes are often in a state of flux (Anning et al. 2006). However, this was not the case in the Dunlean example where a great deal of effort had been put into developing joint systems, common protocols, procedures and documentation. Professionals often raise issues concerning confidentiality, ethics, workload/time problems and professional boundaries that arise when information sharing (Anning et al. 2006, Walker 2008; Jones and Leverett 2008). These issues may have applied in the case of Dunlean (particularly in relation to professional boundaries), so it is important to take a balanced approach to identifying the pressures that the professionals in Dunlean might have been under and that led them to delay the integrated assessment process in a way that led to them having to react to events.

It is possible to contrast the type of reactive information sharing that took place in Dunlean that involves requests for information after an event with proactive information sharing where the service user has already given consent (Walker 2008). The professionals involved in Dunlean could have been more proactive and asked for consent from Molly to seek/share information and established their own roles more quickly. Good partnership requires information to be shared about the roles of professionals (not just about the service user) and the safety/welfare of the child should be the main consideration (Walker 2008).

Information was not shared because the professionals involved failed to recognise the signs that should have started the process of dialogue and information sharing. Even if Molly had not consented to information being collected from other agencies, it is clear that consent for sharing information was not required. That is, consent is not required to share information that is already in the public domain, when a child/adult is at risk of serious harm or when it is required by a legal order (Walker 2008). In this case the initial referral discussion could have led to the case going to the Children's Reporter if Molly had not cooperated. Similarly, the children could have given consent if they were deemed to have the capacity to understand what is being asked, the reasons for sharing information, the alternative choices and could express a consistent/clear view (Walker 2008). In relation to disabled children such as Jenny, it has been argued that professionals should assume that they are competent to put forward a view and that the emphasis should be on professionals to overcome any communication issues that might prevent them from understanding the child's view (Davis and Watson 2000).

Jones and Leverett (2008) have suggested records of consent need to be regularly updated but no professional here checked if there had already been consent given or updated by Molly or the children. The professionals lacked initiative and shared a 'let's monitor' approach that did not pay sufficient attention to local visions concerning integrated working. Dunlean had developed structures to integrated working that aimed to enable more systematic approaches. Yet, we concluded that a lack of clear understanding of these processes, no shared notions of what constitutes an indicator for concern and scant implementation of tools of joint assessment meant that the case had to become very serious before an intervention occurred. This conclusion connects with writing that has argued that there is conflicting evidence as to whether joint assessment forms actually work and too much emphasis has been placed by managers in children and family services on ensuring processes for joint working/regulation are in place rather than making sure that professionals have sufficient knowledge to do their jobs, that their practice/skills are adequate and that children and families experience appropriate outcomes (Munroe 2011).

What would proper assessment and planning have looked like?

The unborn child's requirements should have been addressed in a plan that, for example, ensured Molly attended antenatal appointments, created plans for after the birth and provided support in making preparations for the child's arrival. In the above case the social worker took on the lead professional role and developed the plans with the midwife, GP, health visitor, school staff, voluntary organisations, alcohol specialists and women's aid organisations. Risk management approaches, agreements and plans were established to ensure the children and Molly were not at risk of violence from Derrick (e.g. in the short term Molly agreed they should live with their grandparents). The key aim of the planning process was to ensure that the children felt safe. This required quick identification of protective factors and action to ensure that their situation was changed.

Specific writers encourage you to develop a matrix of assessment in partnership with service users that identifies service users' requirements, the timeframe for providing services, an outline of who will provide the service, how the outcome of the service will be evaluated (e.g. appropriate aims/outcomes are defined) and who the lead person will be (Dolan 2006b). This requires a strong non-judgemental relationship to be developed with service users (Dolan 2006b; Gilligan 2000).

It has been argued that it is important that in multi-professional settings practitioners work to agreed targets, provide advice to local staff, share knowledge (e.g. through joint training with staff/parents/ professionals), carry out joint assessments, clearly articulate what their knowledge base is, work across frontline/preventative/specialist divides, perform home visits, provide joint/targeted working at the community level and actually meet children face to face to uncover their views (Aubrey 2010; Smith and Davis 2010; Davis 2011).

The children's participation in discussions in Dunlean could have utilised the various tools that were established in the Getting It Right for Every Child guidance that included the 'well-being triangle' and resilience matrix (Jack 1997; Daniel and Wassell 2002; Stradling et al. 2008). Some local authorities in Scotland have experienced improved working as a result of carrying out training on the integrated assessment framework, well-being outcomes, the 'my world' triangle and the resilience matrix (Stradling et al. 2009). The triangle provides examples of what a child needs to develop (learning/ achievement, health, confidence, independence, etc.), what they need from those who look after them (guidance, understanding, safety, encouragement, etc.) and what wider-world issues need to be addressed (e.g. resources, housing, schooling, family employment, etc.). The matrix encourages practitioners to unpack children's vulnerability issues (e.g. feeling unsafe in their home), experiences of adverse life events (the arguments and fighting between Molly and Derrick), characteristics of resilience (e.g. Frankie and Jenny had strongly supportive grandparents) and environmental buffers to adversity (the potential to receive support from their peer group, regular attendance at school, membership of local clubs, etc.). Our experience is that training on strengths-based and resilience-based approaches should be much more widespread. However, it should also be noted that standardised tools are only as good as those who use them and that training on such issues should be embedded into real issues from practice (McNicoll et al. 2010).

Activity

What would have happened in this case in your area? What processes/protocols are in place to identify such cases, share information, initiate discussions and enable integrated assessment? Do you think that these approaches are adequate? How could they be improved? What barriers exist that prevent collaboration between professionals and children/families?

Once an assessment has been done, do your planning processes record the reasons for the plan, who is involved in the plan, detailed actions, key issues to be improved, resources to be provided, timescales for change and contingency plans? How do you review the plans? Who leads the review? How often do reviews take place? Does the review record changes of circumstances, information from face-to-face contact, new concerns, the detailed actions that have occurred/have to take place and/or compulsory measures that are required? What criteria does the review measure against (e.g. the outcomes/views of the child, family or professionals)? Does the review discuss any failure to keep agreements/provide services? Is the current level of risk adequately assessed in contrast to previous assessments?

Conclusion

This chapter has discussed policies on assessment, examined the practical context of multi-professional assessment and analysed the case study of Dunlean in order to help you understand the connections between assessment policy, concepts and practice. We have suggested that it is possible for professionals to intervene earlier in family problems; however, we have also suggested that such approaches must be underpinned by politically nuanced strengths-based working (e.g. that develops strong relationships, is clear about the tensions between autonomy/surveillance and balances standardisation with flexibility). We have welcomed processes that attempt to encourage professionals to be accountable, make decisions, have clearly defined procedures, share information, keep records and take action. However, we have also suggested that these processes should be sensitive to the views of children/families, generate local agreements and identify resilience/protective factors in children's lives. Similarly, we have argued that if we are to move away from rigid services that are only concerned with individualistic assessment we have to understand the capacity and limitations of the workforce (particularly in relation to barriers to multi-professional working such as role confusion/entrenchment). This means we should provide more relevant training, develop plans that are realistic, nurture agreements for action that are achievable and regularly review outcomes in order that plans actually result in change.

We have argued that in Dunlean not enough effort was put into face-to-face working, gaining the views of the children and early sharing of information. However, our aim has not been to label the professionals involved – we recognise the difficult conditions within which these professionals work and the fact that many professionals are unaware of contemporary assessment tools, processes and procedures. We would like to conclude by encouraging you to overcome such gaps in knowledge by seeking out the information that you require to do your job. We would also request that you give yourself permission to ask questions of others (particularly when you have concerns). We recognise that it takes courage for professionals to work in new/contemporary ways and that you (like the children/families in Dunlean) are more likely to experience good outcomes when you work in settings that have within them supportive multi-professional relationships. That is, we find it ironic that some organisations and policies promote strengths-based approaches to working with parents/children but do not afford these ideas to professionals. Our final conclusion is that multi-professional working takes place within tense, political and complex environments and therefore we all need to take responsibility for ensuring that deficit ideas are not applied to the children, parents and professionals that inhabit these spaces.

Recommended further reading

Anning, A., Cottrell, D., Frost, N., Green, J. and Robinson, M. (2006) *Developing Multi-professional Teamwork for Integrated Children's Services*. Berkshire: Open University Press.

Dolan, P., Canavan, J., and Pinkerton, J. (eds) (2006) *Family Support as Reflective Practice*. London: Jessica Kingsley.

Stradling, B., MacNeil, M. and Berry, H. (2009) *Changing Professional Practice and Culture To Get It Right for Every Child*. Edinburgh: Scottish Government.

3

Participation and multi-professional working

Chapter Overview

The chapter considers the suggestion that multi-professional working should be more sensitive to the views of children and families. The chapter draws from a case study of the participatory development of a one-point multi-disciplinary children's service in an English local government setting (the case study is included with the kind permission of Liam Cairns at Investing in Children Durham and we wish to acknowledge Liam's support with its development). This chapter examines different definitions of participation that have emerged within Childhood Studies and relates these to different conceptual ideas concerning participation. The chapter outlines different structures of participation that emerged in the Durham case study and that enabled local people to influence decision-making processes. Such structures are contrasted and compared to relational approaches to participation that seek to foster more meaningful collaboration between children, families, professionals and communities. The chapter concludes that when considering the structures, concepts and relationships of participation multi-professional service providers need to balance the use of standardised approaches with the requirement to ensure participatory processes are flexible, provide value diversity and embrace complexity.

Case Study: An integrated one-stop children's service – how to place dialogue with children, young people and families at the heart of one-point services

In 2011 County Durham created a unique opportunity to build the principle of continuous dialogue into the very structure of new children's services teams and centres. They developed a range of approaches to enable the views of children, young people, parents, carers and families to be systematically collected and used to create an agenda for discussion and constant improvement. The process involved collaboration between the local community, a local children's rights organisation (Investing in Children), the local Children's Boards and a schools 360-degree performance development/coaching organisation (Group 8 Education). This partnership focused upon ascertaining what children, young people and families wanted from children's services, making a promise to meet these requirements, meeting regularly and evaluating against those promises. You are encouraged to compare the Durham case with the example of Dunlean from the previous chapter. It is hoped that in so doing you can begin to think how your services can more proactively build strong local relationships and engage with the views of children and families.

Defining our concepts of participation

In the 1990s the sociology of childhood promoted the idea that children were able to take an active part in society (James and Prout 1990). It was argued that children were social agents who though influenced by the structures around them (e.g. schooling, family, economics and politics) could also make an impact on their social world. In particular, this writing encouraged you to question your conceptual hierarchies about children's abilities. Human rights approaches to children and families highlighted the need for professionals to question dated concepts from both psychology and sociology (e.g. the concept of socialisation or the notion of age/stage) that underplayed people's abilities to influence social institutions (e.g. children's services). Such approaches promoted the potential for even the youngest children to possess already formed identities/opinions and requested that practitioners should concentrate on children's and families' abilities rather than their inabilities (Alderson 2000; Davis 2006).

When analysing the case of Dunlean in the previous chapter we connected such ideas to the shift from deficit/individual ideas of children/families to more politically nuanced and ecological approaches. We specifically raised concerns about processes of assessment that did not engage with children's/families' views because they constructed service users as incomplete, irrational and inadequate (Moss et al. 2000; Smith and Davis 2010; Davis 2011). Participation involves listening, working together and change (Davis 2006, 2007, 2011). Politically nuanced strengths-based approaches have at their heart the idea that professionals will listen to other people's points of view and reflect on the possibility that they themselves may misinterpret what children and families are saying. Listening becomes more possible in integrated children's services that are underpinned by the idea that children are agents, have opinions and can take control of their lives (Davis 2011).

Participation and dialogue

Participatory ways of working have sought to engineer a conceptual shift away from the idea that children's services should be concerned with normalisation (processes that aim to create a normal child where parents cannot) and have criticised approaches that define families as abnormal, deficient, weak, in need and as a subject of charity (Moss et al. 2000; Smith and Davis 2010; Davis 2011). In Durham this type of shift was the starting point for their initiative. Children, young people and parents were included from the very start in the design of the new One Point Service. Each One Point Team had regular access to systematic and purposeful information concerning children's, young people's and families' views of the proposed services. The One Point Service involved sustained processes of collaborative dialogue between professionals, parents and children. That is, service users were viewed as agents who could contribute to services in their own community. We can contrast this conceptual starting point with the example of Dunlean where there was little or no initial collaboration between parents and professionals, children were excluded from adult discussions and there was a lack of open dialogue among professionals. Everyday participation was problematic in Dunlean because a culture of listening was lacking. Some authors argue that social spaces such as schools, community centres and leisure/entertainment centres have lacked a culture of dialogue, reflexivity and change, and have been forced (e.g. by a performance indicator culture) into meeting short-term imposed targets at the expense of developing cultures of dialogue and understanding different concepts of participation (Moss and Petrie 2002; Dahlberg et al. 2007; Munroe 2011).

Participation and complexity

While there have been considerable discussions concerning the theory/concepts of participation in academic arenas these have not always been recognised in professional settings (Hill et al. 2004; Davis 2011). Advocates of participation have come from many subject backgrounds (e.g. sociology, geography, community development, child development, cultural psychology, social psychology and environmental psychology) (Malone and Hartung 2010). Within such disciplines there has been an overall journey from theories that have treated children as objects (e.g. who needed to be worked on to meet developmental goals) to more complex approaches that have been concerned with children's inter-subjective relationships within the social spaces they locate (i.e. have perceived children as being able to influence their peers, parents and professionals) (Alderson 2000; Woodhead 2009; Davis 2011).

Investing in Children played an important part in the Durham One Point initiative. As an organisation its staff could draw from many years' experience of interacting with children and service providers and its senior managers have also had substantial experience of debating issues of participation with children, young people, parents, professionals and academics. Investing in Children's practice can be related to a range of academic ideas (Cairns 2001, 2006; Davis 2011). For example, it has recognised and shared the idea that children are capable of making complex decisions (Alderson 1993; Mayall 1994, 1996; Bricher 2001).

Participation and social justice

The One Point initiative had specific aims that connected with academic ideas in the field that suggest that participation projects should have clear goals, enable trust, promote equity and agree targets/outcomes with participants (Lansdown 2001; Cairns 2001, 2006; Davis 2011). Investing in Children has been greatly concerned with the politics of participation. Indeed, they have promoted the idea that participation should lead to real change in people's lives, attend to issues of rights/social justice and be inclusive (Cairns 2001, 2006; Davis 2011).

It has been argued that the concept of social justice is interpreted differently by diverse staff in contrasting organisations (Percy-Smith et al. 2001; Davis 2011). Konstantoni (2011) drew from a range of authors when arguing that:

- social justice was a complex term

- that there were many theories of social justice

- that many of those theories considered both the politics of redistribution (e.g. of rights, duties and resources) and the politics of recognition (e.g. of culture, respect, capacity, etc.) (Vincent 2003; Griffiths 2003; Gewirtz 2006; Riddell 2009)

- that social justice must be understood both in terms of localised everyday stories as well as larger-scale grand narratives (Fraser 1997; Griffiths 2003)

- that social justice was a dynamic, utopian, flexible and temporal thing (Griffiths 2003; Vincent 2003).

In particular, Konstantoni (2011) highlighted the tendency in children's services for concepts of childhood innocence to be utilised as an excuse for neglecting issues of equity and discrimination and for reproducing existing power relations. She called (drawing from Derman-Sparks 1989; Brown 1998; MacNaughton 2000; Robinson and Jones-Diaz 2006) for a shifting of practices towards fairness and social justice that moved beyond 'safe approaches' and promoted a proactive, interventionist and anti-discriminatory stance (Konstantoni 2011). In relation to children and family services other writers drew from Honneth (2000) to define social justice as the person's right to be treated with regard/care, to be entitled to legal rights and to be recognised as having attributes and strengths (Dolan 2006a; Thomas 2009; Davis 2011). Such work connects notions of rights, strengths and thoughtfulness with the need to engage in people's lives, confront thoughtless practice and outline clear expectations regarding the way that people are treated within public services (Davis 2011).

Participation and diverse outcomes

This type of perspective encourages us to question the reasons that services are provided and to analyse the motivation behind providing specific types of provision (e.g. those that enable inclusion, compensate people, are preventative or help develop capacity) (Gilligan 2000; Dolan 2006a; Davis 2011). Processes of participation in children's services can enable greater clarity concerning the different types of services that people require. For example, some people require financial support (redistribution), structural barriers to be removed (e.g. transport, play facilities or housing), information on their rights (e.g. legal advice), their rights to be upheld (e.g. in relation to mistreatment/discrimination) and/or recognition of their own abilities (e.g. respect from professionals that they can contribute to resolving their life issues). This understanding places a duty on service providers not to rigidly assume that any one solution always works and requires concepts such as rights, recognition and respect to be central to multi-professional working (Davis 2011). It also requires much quicker engagement with people's life issues (Davis 2011).

Tensions can arise in participatory processes when too much focus is placed on longer-term aims and hierarchal notions concerning the 'best' types of participation at the expense of working in the present and recognising the context from which a participation process might begin. Longer-term aims can include improved educational capacity, stronger moral foundations, protection from unemployment, prevention of social isolation and improved health (Sinclair and Franklin 2000; Kirby and Bryson 2002; Hogan 2003; Kirby et al. 2003; Davis 2009; Davis 2011). Similarly, some approaches to participation have stressed the hierarchical nature of participation differentiating between approaches that involve children taking leadership roles and those that seek to, for example, manipulate them (e.g. Hart's 1992 ladder of participation). While there is much to be gained from children, parents and local communities running their own projects, processes and services (Davis 2006, 2007, 2011), hierarchical notions of participation have been criticised for their polarity for promoting the assumption that the 'best' forms of participation require participants to be in total charge of a process and for ignoring more sensitive typologies that differentiate between contrasting types of participation on the grounds of their dialogic nature (e.g. listening, supporting expression, taking account of, direct involvement and power sharing) (Shier 2001). These latter types of approach stress the requirement for us to recognise the readiness of service users and caution us to start where people are at and not where we wish them to be.

The Durham initiative was very much underpinned by the recognition of such concepts and the assumption that in any participatory space there will be different types of people with contrasting types of expertise and that no one person (or professional grouping) should be considered to have a monopoly on expert knowledge (Davis 2011). Such a position can form a strong basis from which to build powerful relationships, effective spaces for dialogue and collaborative approaches to delivery (Davis and Hogan 2004; Davis 2007; Davis 2011).

Participation and embedded collaboration

Investing in Children were aware that barriers to participation occurred when children and young people were not involved at the earliest stages of planning, processes were not incremental and approaches did not question issues of power/status (Badham 2000). They wanted to avoid the potential that the process could become tokenistic or open to tokenistic exploitation (Cockburn 1998, 2002; Alderson 2000, 2002; Cairns 2001; Moss and Petrie 2002; Tisdall and Davis 2004; Davis 2011). Tokenism can be avoided by organisations adopting approaches that are consistent and encourage participants to draw on learning from previous initiatives (Badham 2000). Investing in Children drew on their experience of working in Durham to collaboratively plan the participatory process.

Durham Investing in Children had a range of approaches which embedded participation into local practice:

• Investing in Children carried out agenda days and funded children/ young people research teams where children and young people were brought together to discuss ideas, identify issues and investigate possible solutions/best arguments to put to service providers.

• Children and young people don't live in a vacuum, so Investing in Children developed staff development programmes, provided regular newsletters and published examples of different participatory processes in order to increase local understanding.

• Investing in Children encouraged, evaluated and celebrated participatory successful services through its membership scheme. This was open to individuals, teams and projects that could demonstrate they had listened to children and that this listening had resulted in change.

• Investing in Children developed a strategic approach to participation that employed participatory processes to draw together evidence from education, health, social services, etc. of improved outcomes (through participatory processes) for children and young people.

• Investing in Children, through its 'development agency', worked with external partners to develop a 'community of practice' where adults and children and young people were encouraged to learn from each other during participatory processes, projects and events.

Their approach can be contrasted with participation processes that are instigated in local authorities and at national level in a cynical attempt to legitimise situations where top-down decisions have already been made. In such cases participation has been criticised for being more of a manipulative tool than a theoretical framework and for being a tokenistic false therapy for experiences that require more fundamental change (Pupavac 2002; Malone and Hartung 2010). Indeed, politicians have been criticised for manipulating the idea of service user choice in ways that result in lots of people being asked their opinion who have not actually used services in a first-hand way or in ways that produce a single reduced/limited set of aims (based on the service provider's own idea of what the problem is) when a variety of services and outcomes is what service users require (Seddon 2008).

The Durham initiative attempted to avoid tokenism by stimulating fundamental change concerning the relationships between service user and provider. However, the professionals involved did not assume that participation was a panacea to all their organisational ills or that it was free from internal contradictions. Indeed, well intentioned participatory processes can often have little impact on public decision-making (Cairns 2001, 2006; Kirby and Bryson 2002; Davis 2011). Writers from systems theory have questioned pseudo-participatory, market and consumerist approaches to participation that have promoted private sector notions that competition between providers can better meet customer needs and choices.

Marketisation perspectives promoted the idea that service users should have choice and flexibility (Farnham and Horton 1996; Pierson 2004). It was argued that a 'purchaser' of services (e.g. parents choosing their child's school or a patient choosing a hospital) should be able to move their 'custom' between providers (Pierson 2004: 157). Farnham and Horton (1996: 3) suggested that market systems became preferred to politics as a means of allocating resources and distributing welfare because they were believed to offer personal freedom (e.g. where people could choose services that closely met their own personal needs). This shift led to a redefinition of the concept of welfare from the idea that the task of states was to provide citizens with a safety net of benefits to the notion that welfare (as part of a wider market) should promote public interest, economic progress, work and wealth (Brown 2003; Giddens 2004).

However, the pursuit of lower costs and profits often led to cheaper provision, poorer services and lower customer satisfaction and therefore it was recommended that public services should avoid participatory approaches based on manipulated choice (e.g. that ask voters to decide which service should be cut rather than whether there should be cuts) (Seddon 2008). Public service providers were encouraged to develop more systematic participatory approaches that reduced the need for cuts by adopting approaches that removed waste and by ensuring that service users get their problems solved as early as possible (Seddon 2008). The next section considers what a more systematic approach to participation looks like in terms of the structures that underpinned the Durham process.

 Activity

Investing in Children publish reports of their work on their website. It is possible for organisations to commission reports but fail to act on them and/or review their progress. Can you look at their reports or reports from participatory processes in your area to identify the issues that children and families have raised? Can you consider the pros and cons of the reports? What does this tell you about the nature of participation in your area? Can you analyse your own way of working? How does your conceptual starting point compare with that of the Durham case study? Does your organisation welcome service users' views? Are service users listened to in a proactive and systematic way? Do you have any fears concerning working in a participatory way with children and families? Can you talk these over with colleagues or people with experience of participation?

Structures of participation

The Dunlean case study demonstrated that acute situations arise if concepts of listening and dialogue are not put into practice. The Durham process collaboratively developed and scrutinised the structures of participation with service users (Kirby et al. 2003). When developing their strategy for instigating the multi-professional community-based participatory process in Durham, participants considered a range of factors including the speed at which the innovation should occur, the swiftness with which the strategies should become embedded and the processes by which learning would be exchanged and reinforced. At the centre of this consideration was the issue of how much time and funding was available for staff, children and young people to collaborate on learning. Some participatory processes are costly and time-consuming (e.g. requiring fund-raising and budget allocation) which is a reason why they need to be well thought out in terms of their aims and outcomes (Badham 2000; Gabriel 1998; Children's Society 2000; Seddon 2008; Davis 2011).

Participation resources

Investing in Children's processes are underpinned by the perspective that genuine participation involves working on well resourced (e.g. in terms of time, funding and commitment) processes that concentrate on issues of real relevance to children themselves (Lansdown 2001). The types of resources that Investing in Children put into processes of participation include allocation of staff time, payment for participants' travel costs and other expenses, the provision of meals, drinks and snacks, and the production of reports, presentation materials and web spaces. In previous processes of participation children and families had suggested to Investing in Children that they wanted services to be more modern, leaner, quicker and responsive and to move beyond rigid rules to enable the development of local collaborative problem-solving (Davis 2011).

Well-structured, participatory, integrated and multi-professional services can actually be very cost-effective if they prevent duplication of effort by avoiding service users having to repeat their stories to a never-ending succession of professionals, by agreeing/improving processes of information-sharing that reduce the time spent on initial assessment and enabling the earlier generation of low-cost solutions (Seddon 2008; Davis 2011). A central aim of policy development on multi-professional working in children and family services has been to reduce the proportion of children experiencing child protection processes by supporting families much earlier with their life issues (Aldgate and Tunstill 1995; Tisdall 1995; McGhee and Waterhouse 2002; Glenny and Roaf 2008; Walker 2008). It is argued that more participatory and proactive interventions should lead to the prevention of crisis situations in the lives of children and families and for money to be saved on later-stage, higher and more costly interventions (DfES 2004a; Brown and White 2006).

It should be noted that such financial savings do not materialise when we simply instigate top-down structural change to integrated services. For example, in the early days of national calls for more integrated approaches to be adopted in children and family services it was argued that new polices would bring great savings. However, research indicated that progress on costs was slow and inconsistent and that while lots of children received a wide range of services they were largely uncoordinated and lacked an overall assessment of the child's requirements (Scottish Executive 2001; DoH 2003; Munroe 2011). For example, it was argued that too much focus was placed on policies at the expense of developing workers' understandings concerning practice (Munroe 2011). We can see the consequences of weak practices of assessment in the Dunlean case study (Chapter 2) where the case lacked participation and led to a resource-intensive intervention.

Participation, policy and power

When analysing processes of assessment in Dunlean we suggested that national policies had encouraged the local authority to improve services and make them more participatory by enabling more clearly structured and systematic approaches to assessment, planning and delivery. Yet the complex structural nature of participation meant that local staff had not recognised that their approach involved practices that created barriers to participation because they deemed children to be less powerful than adults (Hart 1992; Chawala 2001; Malone and Hartung 2010). Staff failed to utilise forms of interaction, commitment and listening that examined the power relations of participation (Shier 2001). This meant that staff and service users had not examined their different roles within the participation process (e.g. whether they were manipulators, collaborators, facilitators, planners, co-researchers, co-managers, autonomous leaders, etc.) (Hart 1992; Davis and Hogan 2004; Malone and Hartung 2010).

At a community level participation has been seen to encounter problems with disengaged local environments (e.g. due to poverty, crime, poor housing), weak local organisations (e.g. with staff who lack training, funding or policies), underdeveloped community/ social organisation (e.g. few informal social, supportive or bridging networks) and a lack of community connectedness (e.g. a lack of connection between community leaders, service users and local systems) (Chaskin 2006).

Dunlean had policies of participation but these had not been embedded fully into structures and cultures. Staff in Dunlean had yet to consider their conceptual starting point from which to build participatory structures in their services. The range of starting points could have included romantic beliefs that children should plan their own lives without adults, the representative objective that participation should involve specific professionals/children acting as advocates, the bureaucratic/institutional perception that participation should be about uncovering needs for future service planning, the individualistic aim that structures should be about specific people's rights, and the proactive participatory principle that connects the need for vision with the need to change (Francis and Lorenzo 2002; Malone and Hartung 2010). The lack of a clear strategy in Dunlean can be contrasted with the approach in Durham which developed a specific structure of participation based on partnership and checks/balances.

At a conceptual level, service providers, children and families require to be able to clearly articulate/understand the thinking behind a participatory process and work thorough any confusion caused by tensions concerning what the aims of the services are, e.g. participatory (to be based on service users views), 'social integrationist' (to help people get jobs), moral (to stop bad things happening in families and communities or to judge/intervene when events happen), redistributive (to provide service users with resources) or social dynamic (to combine all of these and develop collaborative complex approaches that interrogate the meaning and politics of everyday interactions within services) (Davis 2007, 2011).

Participation procedures

The Durham initiative sought to develop a dynamic approach that balanced out formal and informal ideas. Investing in Children have been critical of formal approaches such as representative structures (e.g. school councils, local government forums and youth parliaments) for duplicating the failings of adult democratic structures (Cairns 2001). It has been argued that such structures can often result in gaps emerging between the local population and representatives, act as a barrier to local collaborative dialogue and therefore fail to stimulate long-term change (Alderson 2002; Kirby and Bryson 2002; Hogan 2003; Davis and Hogan 2004; Cairns 2006; Turkie 2010). A central principle of the One-Point Services development project was that effective services should sensitively meet families' requirements, respond to their circumstances and enable families to make better use of provision. It was concluded that such a shift in service organisation needed new arrangements that involved service providers developing genuine and robust mechanisms for engagement and participation with service users.

Participation processes involve procedures that occur within specific structures (e.g. through membership of governing bodies, recruitment panels, management committees, advisory boards, steering groups, forums, meetings, conferences, research projects and news groups) (Gabriel 1998; Badham 2000). They can also involve different organisational structures such as conferences, residential weekends, forums, draft plans and committees and different forms of media (e.g. publications, presentations, videos, training packs, websites, campaigns and editing written material) (Gabriel 1998; Badham 2000; TCS 2000; Davis 2011). Similarly, participatory approaches can be targeted to specific issues or include collaboration with people across different levels/sectors in organisations (e.g. staff, senior managers, policy-makers, local politicians and national executives/policy-makers) (Gabriel 1998; Badham 2000; TCS 2000; Tisdall and Davis 2004; Davis 2011). In Durham processes of participation benefited from linking the agenda of children and families to service level agreements, information-sharing events and the development of local multi-professional protocols (Percy-Smith et al. 2001; Cairns 2006). In the case of the One Stop children's teams and centres, staff/managers introduced ideas from discussions between children, parents and practitioners into the performance management approach of the local service. It has been argued that such collaborative processes increase the power and influence of children, young people and families (Percy-Smith et al. 2001; Cairns 2006).

In Durham a specific work stream (led by Investing in Children and supported by the Local Children's Boards) was created that ensured that children and families were part of the process of service design. Spaces were created for children, young people, parents and carers to come together, first on their own and then with key project staff, to discuss their ideas about what would make the new service most successful. For example, over an 18-month period, around 300 children and young people and 50 parents contributed to the design of the new service.

The Durham approach was well thought through; however, the Dunlean case study encourages us to question the limitations of the people involved in multi-professional decision-making processes. Multi-professional settings have gained a lot from participatory processes that have embraced notions of complexity and enabled professionals (and others) to question the type of lassez-faire and deficit approaches that excluded the children in Dunlean (Davis 2011). Participatory structures such as those developed by the Durham One Stop Service aim to enable organisations to take a more systemic approach to service planning, design and delivery. Such approaches have been found to be able to deliver more relevant multi-professional services that are based on children's/families' requirements. They have also been found to boost staff morale by increasing their sense of connectedness to colleagues/service users, to increase productivity/effectiveness because staff have greater clarity concerning their work aims and to promote creativity/innovation by intensifying processes of dialogue/learning that can stimulate new thinking (Kirby and Bryson 2002; Hogan 2003; Davis 2011).

Participation, standardisation and flexibility

In the Durham One Stop Service agreements and standards were developed to enshrine changes. This included parents and children commenting on the proposed locations of the new centres, making clear statements of their expectations of the One Stop Teams and co-creating a 'Pledge' document for staff and managers to sign up to. This document was accepted and endorsed by staff, unions and the Integrated Services Development Programme Board. It was also incorporated into job descriptions for posts within the new One Stop centres/teams. The document included the commitment that staff would:

- treat service users with respect and listen/value their opinions

- ask service users where they wanted to meet and give three hours notice of cancellations

- ask service users how they wanted to be contacted and discuss with the service users any need to contact a parent, carer, relative or other person

- put what they have agreed to do in writing, give the service user a copy and let them know if agreements could not be kept

- put children's and young people's priorities at the top of the list

- enable children, young people and parents to be involved in recruiting, interviewing and selecting staff

- make service users aware of compliment and complaint processes and always listen, act upon and respond (within five working days) with information to every complaint

- never reject/turn away a child, young person or parent from a hub

- 'hold the baton', e.g. never say they can't help or let/make a service user leave until they are happy with the help they have been given.

The thinking behind the process was very clear. Children and families were perceived to have a right to participate in local decision-making. People assumed that the planning process would be improved by involving them at the start and that the service would be better tailored to their requirements. Children and parents were believed to be potentially as powerful as service providers, to possess their own types of expertise (e.g. concerning knowledge of their own social worlds) and an attempt was made to enshrine the change of traditional power relationships into contracts and agreements. This process had to balance ideas of standardisation with issues of diversity and flexibility. They did so by having formal agreements on the nature of service provision and relationships without actually specifically defining what service outcomes would be. That is, the Durham approach enshrined concepts of participatory trust, respect and dialogue in procedures that would enable flexible outcomes to emerge.

The proactive nature of the Durham One Point Service can be contrasted with the reactive process in Dunlean. The One Point Service had integrated concepts of participation into its structures in a much more systematic way than was the case in Dunlean. The multi-professional teams in Durham aimed to establish local relationships, discover what service users wanted, examine the processes/barriers that prevent delivery and change them, based on dialogue between staff and service users. The previous chapter concluded that staff in Dunlean needed to be more systematic in their approach. The processes in Durham sought to be more systematic by defining the structures and standards of participation. However, it also recognised that the outcomes of participation would be complex and dependent on context.

It is important for you to realise that there can be benefits for participants when participatory processes have clearly understood structures, but this does not mean that such processes need to have fixed outcomes. The specific or desired outcome of the participatory processes can be flexible and do not always have to produce a product (e.g. a consumerist object). Outcomes that service users such as children and young people want can include recognition of perceived injustices (in a political sense), relational change in their local area (for more say in service development or greater consideration given to family members) or for local problems to be collaboratively unpacked (for processes of conflict resolution to occur between themselves and other parties) (Davis 2011).

Participatory structures are only as good as their ethos, hence, if they are characterised by rigid rules/hierarchy, then it is unlikely that grassroots ideas will be given credence (Percy-Smith et al. 2001; Kirby et al. 2003). Indeed, participatory processes can do more harm than good particularly when participants feel let down by processes of listening where ideas for change are not fulfilled (Borland et al. 2001; Dorrian et al. 2001; Tisdall and Davis 2004). In Durham the partnership between service users and providers clearly investigated why and how they would develop a participatory process. They very much wanted to deal with issues in the present and the process followed the perspective that service providers should enable individuals, families, groups and communities to define the scope of the participatory processes (Gabriel 1998; Davis 2007). There was also a perception that by beginning the initiative by developing solid local processes, children and families would benefit in the future (yet note that the initiative did not over-define what that future would be).

Systems theorists have encouraged us to think of service users' needs in the present and to create dialogue that has enabled service users to set the form, function and outcomes of services (Seddon 2008). In so doing, they have recommended that service providers engage with issues of diversity because they believe that a lack of opportunity to develop complex solutions leads to service users receiving services they do not want (Seddon 2008). Similarly, it has been argued that notions of distributional justice (the idea that power can be shared between diverse people) encourage us to restrict the use of standardisation in the public service (Dahlberg et al. 2007). At the centre of this perspective is the idea that equality of service provision is a diverse concept and that the principle of equal treatment when rigidly imposed in services can result in the suppression of difference (e.g. the use of a 'one size fits all' approach). In particular it has been argued that notions of equality do not mean that everyone should be the same and that the usefulness of a specific service provision is open to cultural interpretation (Young 1990; Thomas 2009). This type of writing calls for a recognition of a politics of difference (where the individual service user or professional is not reduced to one identity but has multiple identities across different contexts) and the realisation that the ways that institutions define and attempt to resolve people's life problems can in themselves become further sources of exclusion

(Penna and O'Brien 1996). These ideas suggest that we should balance the need for formal participatory structures with the need to have flexible processes of dialogue (Percy-Smith et al. 2001; Cairns 2006).

The requirement for structural flexibility means there can be no uniform approach to children and family life issues and that processes of participation (like processes of assessment) have to realistically take account of issues such as worker capacity, training requirements, local agreements and existing structures/relationships (Malone and Hartung 2010; Davis 2011). In particular, participation has been seen to fail on an individual capacity level because of a lack of staff: skills, resources, enjoyment, motivation, opportunities, commitment, planning, relevance and willingness to work with service users of different ages/backgrounds (Gilligan 2000; Moss and Petrie 2002; Prout et al. 2006).

Individual issues can be as important as structural issues when understanding the requirement of flexible participation. This perspective puts an obligation on you as practitioners to recognise that participation can take place in a range of formal and informal settings, e.g. families (ordinary family processes and legal family processes such as divorce/care), public services (schooling), public spaces (neighbourhoods), commercial settings (shops, entertainment, sports and leisure facilities), young people's groups (clubs, voluntary organisations, traditional charities, children's rights/participatory organisations, etc.), pseudo-democratic institutions (children's councils, youth parliaments, forums, etc.) and institutions/processes that traditionally exclude children and young people (parliaments to which people are elected and represent others) (Thomas 2007, 2009).

The school staff in Dunlean failed to carry out the simplest form of informal participation (asking the children their views). They only carried out cursory multi-professional discussions (as part of existing work processes) and could have shared more in-depth information (that was already known to various services) at an earlier stage. In the most part formal participatory processes, policies and structures will not always be successful. These can lead to a very limited number of outcomes because participation is difficult and is complicated by human relations, local politics and opportunist manipulation (Cockburn 1998, 2002; Alderson 2000, 2002; Cairns 2001; Moss and Petrie 2002; Tisdall and Davis 2004; Davis 2011). The next section discusses in more depth human relational aspects of participation.

Activity

Does the call to balance flexible and standardised approaches to participation raise any issues in your workplace? For example, are your structures, concepts and ethos of participation complementary? It is very difficult to create decentralised structures that balance rules with flexibility. Is participation in your workplace an informal part of everyday processes or is it associated with rules? How helpful are the structures of participation in your workplace? Ideas from systems theory encourage us to build our strategies outside in from the service users' points of view. Can you discuss with colleagues and service users how this might occur in your services?

Participatory relationships

Investing in Children has encountered a range of problems when trying to develop local relationships (Cairns 2001). In particular it has met resistance from organisations who feel that only they have the particular skills set to work with specific service users (e.g. young people from specific communities, groups that experience deprivation or different age groups). This is often a problem in multi-professional services (that some professionals create demarcated boundaries around service users). It is important that we avoid stigmatising such people and work out ways to built supportive relationships that bridge to practitioners who have concerns about participation.

Participation and interrelational problem solving

It has been argued that organisations have to have a coherent set of policies and principles in place to enable joined-up thinking, that learning from participatory practice should influence organisational development and that processes of dialogue and joint learning should be developed that reduce the barriers between different layers of organisations and stimulate cross-organisational exchange, cultures of cooperation and structural decentralisation (Percy-Smith et al. 2001).

Some writers have found that parents and children are keen to be involved in service development/delivery and that it depends on the context of their lives (Davis and Hancock 2007; Davis 2011). It is important that we do not undervalue the latent reserves of wisdom, energy and compassion that exist within local areas (Cockburn 2010). Indeed, early intervention in local issues requires a more integrated and relational approach to problem-solving (Aldgate and Tunstill 1995; Tisdall 1997; McGhee and Waterhouse 2002; Glenny and Roaf 2008; Walker 2008).

Dunlean appeared to lack a relational approach to problem-solving. This can be contrasted to examples in Durham where Investing in Children have resourced processes that have helped children and young people to develop relationships with planners, commissioners and service providers concerning issues such as mental health, libraries, transport, youth clubs, health programmes and disability (Cairns 2001, 2006; Davis 2011). The process of building relationships in the Durham One Stop Service initiative involved the development of children's and parents' groups in each of the five localities of the children's centres. Throughout the development participants voiced a commitment, willingness and expectation that they would continue to be involved in dialogue beyond the start-up of the new service. For example, the processes set up a future structure for dialogue including regular meetings, family-centred evaluation, clear recording/reporting of issues, active responsiveness and sustained participation:

- *Meetings.* Quarterly 'agenda day' meetings enabled service users and providers to discuss what approaches were going well and what needed to be improved.

- *Evaluation.* Questionnaires were carried out with staff and structured interviews were carried out with children, young people and parents to establish individual and aggregate performance.

- *Reports.* Documents recorded issues that arose in the agenda day meetings and evaluation process. The team manager and staff were tasked with analysing and responding to these documents. Meetings were carried out with Group 8 to enable the analysis of evaluation findings with the children, young people and parents.

- *Responsiveness.* The team manager regularly met with staff in team and management meetings and with children, young people and parents in local meetings to debate and agree plans to address issues that were raised.

- *Sustained participation.* One Point Teams agreed to regularly gather evidence of transformation in order to be able to annually renew their Investing in Children membership. (Investing in Children membership is only awarded to organisations that can demonstrate they have enabled ongoing processes of participation, dialogue and change.)

This process sought to build trust by reducing the social space between children's families, community members and staff.

Participation and community relationships

A number of writers in childhood studies have highlighted the interconnected rather than autonomous rights of individuals (Cockburn 1998; Davis 2011). In some organisations appreciative and cooperative enquiry has enabled insiders and outsiders to develop a collaborative approach to a point where the boundaries are blurred between service user and provider. For example, children's centres in Sheffield have developed a structure where community members can begin as service users, become volunteers who support others and subsequently be employed as staff members (Broadhead et al. 2008). Similarly, in Canada the boundaries between service provider and user were blurred by joint training initiatives that encouraged local service users to become providers and to conceptualise, define and deliver local integrated services (Ball and Sones 2004; Moore et al. 2005).

In other communities participatory appraisal has been utilised to ensure that the ways that organisations listen do not create barriers to participation and actually build fruitful relationships (McKenzie 2010). Participatory appraisal employed a range of techniques including visual material (photography, mapping, timelines, scaling, etc.), dialogue (interviews/focus groups) and feedback (learning cycles) to evolve key questions, ideas and meanings from participants' perspectives (McKenzie 2010).

These approaches stretch the notion of relationships beyond the boundaries of a multi-disciplinary team of professionals and service users to include community members. Such approaches have enabled service providers to increase the pool of people who can be considered to have expert knowledge and can deliver services (including children, young people, parents, relatives and community members) (Davis 2000; Moore et al. 2005). Such approaches have been based on the assumption that service users, professionals and community members have a variety of sets of cultural knowledge/competence and therefore that relationship building can enable such diverse ideas to underpin service development (Moore et al. 2005).

In respect to processes of assessment in Dunlean we argued that it was important that practitioners felt free to work on outcomes with children, families and communities, to build trust, dispel preconceptions and develop processes that were responsive to local views. This argument connects with literature on participation that proposes that the relational aspects of participation should be utilised to enable local people to have more control over their community, to utilise local resources/strengths to reduce dependency on outsiders, and to enable responsibility for better outcomes to be widely shared (Maitney 1997; Percy-Smith et al. 2001). In Durham Investing in Children drew from the idea that discursive spaces can be established where children and adults work through what participation and inclusion means in local contexts (Cockburn 2002; Moss and Petrie 2002). The success of collaborative and relational approaches has very much been linked to the ability of practitioners to be perceived as warm, caring and trusting (Glenny and Roaf 2008). It has also been argued that in order for relational approaches to flourish in multi-disciplinary services relational approaches should include an understanding of the benefits of analysing conflict (Davis 2011). For example, it is important that local traditions/differences between service users are considered when we try to establish collaborative service development (Broadhead et al. 2008; Leverett 2008) and to recognise that barriers to collaborative multi-professional working can occur when service providers are not able to resolve problems within their own ways of working (e.g. in-fighting between services has created barriers to participation for parents and children) (Smith and Davis 2010).

Participation as a well thought through process

Investing in Children has been part of events (funded by the Economic and Social Research Council) where service users, academics, practitioners and policy-makers have analysed processes of participation (Hill et al. 2004). These events resulted in a much more enlightened perspective of participation and a document co-constructed by participants that suggested participation should aim to:

- provide a range of opportunities for children, young people, families and communities to be involved

- ensure that the voices of children and young people are heard equally as those of adults

- create opportunities for two-way dialogue between children, young people, adults and decision-makers

- be concerned with the lived lives of children and young people, for example, the issues that young people agree are important to them

- recognise that participation is more than a means to an end. It should not be an end in itself, rather it should enable children and young people to make things better in their lives

- enable children and young people to participate on their own terms (not simply satisfy the expectations of the adult community) and reverse the usual trend of adults deciding what they think is best for children and young people

- be transformative, for example by challenging the perspective that children and young people are lacking the knowledge or competence to be participants and by making mental health services more relevant, effective and safe for children and young people.

(Davis and Edwards eds. 2004)

At the heart of this collaborative and relational approach to participation is the notion that participation is not a single project, it is a sustainable process (Davis 2011). Social activities such as intra-project visits, team-building events, events facilitated by external experts, practice development forums, reflective circles and workshops for exchanging practice have all been recommended as a way of embedding participatory practice (Maitney 1997). Investing in Children has been adept at utilising such collaborative processes to ensure that there has been consistent and sustained engagement with children and families in Durham. They have utilised collaborative relational approaches to:

- produce and implement local strategies/plans that are based on outcomes, not scientific/abstract targets/indicators

- develop a systematic approach to service development

- create pathways of communication and feedback between, within and outwith services

- develop training, monitoring and evaluation to support the implementation of the local collaborative service development

- balance staff concerns over the practical aspects of collaborative working with the need to establish a culture of participation that builds collaborative relationships across multi-professional services

- encourage managers/staff to practise what they preach at all levels within their organisation

- respond to difficulties when they arise, overcome conflict and focus on outcomes not arguments

- overcome reluctance from staff, service users, leaders and managers to have open discussions.

Their experience suggests that staff and managers in Dunlean should have at an earlier stage put their energies into questioning power/hierarchy in their multi-professional services, developing collaborative/relational local processes of participation, analysing/rethinking their children's services systems, encouraging evaluation without fear of criticism/reprisal and providing staff with time to consider the pros and cons of their own and other people's perspectives without fear of criticism or reprisal. That is, though staff had received training on holistic assessment (which included the idea they should listen to children), they had not been encouraged to examine in depth how participatory their relationships, cultures and systems were.

Participatory approaches are problematic when people do not want to participate, structures can encourage a dependency culture (rather than shift power relations) and service providers can assume children and young people are insufficiently informed to make complex decisions (Maitney 1997). Individual and collective leadership is required to turn such perspectives around. Literature has argued that participatory processes are most likely to achieve good outcomes when organisations have a clear vision, experienced leadership and the processes are supported at senior levels (Cutler and Taylor 2003). We would encourage you to view the concept of leadership as complex and to examine closely your role in leading a participatory agenda in your organisation. At worst you should be able to work on your relational approaches to participation during your face-to-face engagements with children and families. Whatever your position in your organisation the first step towards participation begins with listening more closely to the views of the people you interact with on a daily basis (Davis 2011).

 Activity

What approaches are used in your workplace for building relationships of participation? Have you encountered resistance to building such relationships? Can you discuss these issues with colleagues/service users? Are you aware of the different tools (e.g. participatory appraisal) that can be utilised to facilitate dialogue and relationship building? Can you consider their pros and cons? Do you have relationships with non-public-sector organisations that have experience of participation? What steps have you taken to ensure that people from diverse backgrounds can participate in decision-making processes?

Conclusion

This chapter has demonstrated the need for service providers to make explicit the theories/concepts that underpin their participatory processes. It has contrasted approaches that recognise children and parents as social actors with those that underplay their abilities. It has highlighted the thinking behind the One Stop Service participatory process, for example that children and families are capable of making complex decisions, that participation can enable them to collaboratively define the outcomes they want from services and that services should be established on the basis of trust, equity and dialogue. This chapter has encouraged you to engage with the politics of participation and to be clear about the aims (e.g. redistribution, social justice, rights, recognition and fairness), outcomes (e.g. inclusion, respect, compensation, development and prevention), structures (e.g. advocacy services, planning groups, community-based initiatives, standards, protocols, service level agreements, committees, work streams) and relationships (conversational, listening, communicative, conflicting, cooperative, dependent, power sharing, 'expert', learning, caring, trusting, warm, co-constructive, collaborative, transformative, voluntary, formal and informal) of participation.

We have encouraged you to think about issues of timing, choice and hierarchy and concluded that if we are to build sustainable participatory structures and relationships we need to begin participatory processes from where people are (rather than where we want them to be), recognise the diverse expertise of all participants (not simply professionals) and avoid tokenism (e.g. setting up processes that cannot change anything).

The chapter demonstrated Investing in Children's experience at developing participatory processes and their ability to underpin their developments with consistent approaches (e.g. related to resources, training, recognition/membership and reporting/ publishing). Investing in Children's approach was contrasted with more manipulative processes such as one of cost-cutting exercises and pseudo-participatory approaches (e.g. school councils).

This chapter also demonstrated a tension between informal and formal outcomes, structures and relationships of multi-disciplinary working. We encouraged you to recognise the limitations of hierarchical approaches and concluded that it is important for you to engage with service users as early as possible and balance their requirements in the present with their/your aspirations for the future. In so doing, this chapter contrasted reactive and proactive approaches to participation and encouraged you to adopt more systemic approaches including clear/consistent aims, processes and practices.

However, the chapter also recognised that participation occurs at different levels and we concluded that when considering the structures, concepts and relationships of participation service providers need to balance the use of standardised approaches with the requirement to ensure participatory processes are flexible, value diversity and embrace complexity. Similarly, we concluded that the most important form of participation can simply involve face-to-face informal discussions, that the first stage of any participatory process should be to find out how children, young people and families want to participate, and therefore that processes of dialogue within multi-professional services should be built on an examination of concepts of power, cooperation and decentralisation.

Recommended further reading

Cairns, L. (2006) 'Participation with purpose', in K. Tisdall, J. Davis, M. Hill and A. Prout (eds), *Children, Childhood and Social Inclusion*. London: Policy Press.

Hill, M,. Davis, J., Proat, A. and Tisdall K. (eds) (2004) 'Children, young people and participation', *Children and Society*, 18 (2): 77–176.

Kirby, P. with Bryson, S. (2002) *Measuring the Magic? Evaluating Young People's Participation in Public Decision-making*. London: Carnegie Young People Initiative.

4

Traditional structures of multi-professional leadership and management

Chapter Overview

The previous chapter suggested that multi-professional participatory processes involve a tension between hierarchical and individual ideas. It suggested that participation processes should balance structural with relational approaches, that participatory leadership involved a complex interplay between issues of hierarchy and dialogue and that relational processes of participation could enable leadership to be exercised collaboratively. This chapter examines in more depth individual, hierarchical and relational notions of leadership/management and encourages you to examine the structures and relationships in your workplace. It questions ideas concerning individual leadership (visionary leaders/change agents), standardised management (uniform approaches), professional hierarchy (conflict over roles) and marketisation (service user choice). It connects ideas of choice and flexibility to human relational notions of leadership and concludes that the spaces where we work are never static, that processes of power in organisations can be fluid and therefore that organisations should include a balance of individual and collective approaches. The central aim of the chapter is to help you understand the restrictions of traditional hierarchical types of leadership and management and to begin to engage with relational approaches. In order to achieve this the chapter draws on a case study of the development of an integrated children and family service in Pentesk local authority in Scotland to highlight how hierarchical approaches to multi-professional working can cause tensions between colleagues.

Case Study: A multi-disciplinary children and family service

The case study examines the development of a multi-professional children and family service that introduced integration teams into a Scottish local authority (we have given the local authority the pseudonym Pentesk). The strategic plan for the process aimed to enable local development of:

- children's services as a single service system
- a joint children's services plan
- inclusive access to universal services
- coordinated needs assessment and solution-focused approaches
- coordinated intervention and targeted services.

This initiative emerged at a time when services in Pentesk involved little integration, yet, policy guidance was calling on local authorities in Scotland to move towards greater multi-professional working in the hope that such initiatives could improve outcomes for children, young people and families (Smith 2009). The case study of Pentesk is employed in this chapter to discuss issues concerning styles of leadership/management, processes of decision-making and issues of multi-professional conflict/hierarchy. We hope that our analysis of the experience of managers and staff in Pentesk will enable you to consider the context of children's services/organisations in your local areas, to analyse your own experience of organisational management and to consider possible contradictions in relation to multi-professional leadership/management concepts, structures and relationships.

Concepts of visionary leadership and management

A management structure was established in Pentesk that aimed to promote local multi-professional dialogue between a range of services on issues of assessment, planning and delivery. This structure involved a children's services planning group (including heads/directors of services and members of the community planning group), different professional groupings (integrated, link and extended teams) and various professionals adopting different levels of management responsibility. It was hoped that key managers could act as visionary change agents and would motivate others to adopt more integrated and multi-professional approaches. That is, managers in community learning/development, education, health and social work came to the conclusion that leadership by key individuals was required if Pentesk children and family services were to move to more integrated ways of working and to stimulate more systematic multi-professional working. This approach was in keeping with ideas discussed in the previous chapter that argued that participatory structures could benefit from a clear vision, experienced leadership and support at senior levels (Cutler and Taylor 2003). Such approaches characterise managers as key people who can set the vision for others based on their individual ability to rationalise problems and promote solutions (Katz and Kahn 1966; Armstrong 2009).

Such ideas connect processes of change to notions of individual leadership. You should recognise that there is no universally accepted definition of leadership or management and that professionals' perspectives of these terms alter depending on the context they find themselves in (Jeffree and Fox 1998; Lawler and Bilson 2010). For example, your approach as a leader may relate to your influence, creativity, emotional generosity and/or role, whereas a manager may have been appointed to a particular position (Jeffree and Fox 1998; Lawler and Bilson 2010). This distinction is similar to the idea that leaders draw their power from, for example, position (legitimate power), influence (coercive power), personal gain (reward power), reputational (referent power) and professional knowledge (expert power) (French and Raven 1986; Lawler and Bilson 2010). Such conceptual divisions separate out leadership based on relationships (e.g. trust, inspiration, support, direction) with leadership based on more formal management roles that involve you taking organisational responsibility (e.g. for people, plans, performance and resources) (Lawler and Bilson 2010).

We can see this distinction in policies regarding multi-professional working. In Chapter 2 we outlined the policy themes that aimed to promote a fundamental change in the way in which children's and family services were delivered. Policies recommended a radical change to the way service providers operated within the UK (e.g. in relation to single service delivery). There was an expectation that children and families would receive more proactive service delivery based on an integrated front-line assessment/delivery, integrated strategies/ planning and multi-professional governance (Scottish Government 2001; DfES 2004).

At the centre of this approach was the idea that it is possible to make specific people responsible for service processes and outcomes (e.g. the named person and lead professional). Such ideas can be connected to rational objective approaches of management that reify the rational ability of individual managers (viewing them as autonomous/ independent analysts), promote the concept of heroic management (believing they are people who are leading us with vision to a better place) and encourage us to adopt transferable, rational and linear management strategies (to iron out uncertainty, inefficiency and diversity (Lawler and Bilson 2010)).

Such ideas can be found in both the private and public sector when people assume that the leader is the most important person in an organisation and/or stress the importance of leaders' individual traits, actions, attitudes and characteristics (Bolden et al. 2003). For example, proponents of 'Great Man' (Carlyle 1869) and 'Trait Theory' have suggested that your actions are connected to your ability to act as a heroic leader (e.g. in a time of crisis) or to act as a technical expert who can apply scientific methods to the design and redesign of work tasks. Such theories have been concerned with your innate leadership qualities and your ability to maximise efficiencies, motivate workers and simplify processes. Trait Theory specifically encouraged managers to work on aspects of their personality including honesty, integrity, desire to lead, confidence, judgement, knowledge, creativity, flexibility, charisma and emotional intelligence (Bolden et al. 2003; Grint 2005; Lawler and Bilson 2010). Writers who promoted this theory (e.g. Cattell 1963) created the idea that the manager had specific traits that should not vary over time, change in different situations or alter depending on who the manager was interacting with. Such perspectives have connected notions of management and leadership with charisma/personality, authority and forcefulness (Bolden et al. 2003; Armstrong 2009; Lawler and Bilson 2010). They have also emphasised the negative aspects of ambiguity, arguing that good leaders/managers ensured that roles are clear and compatible (Katz and Kahn 1966; Armstrong 2009). At the centre of this way of thinking is the idea that you (as the manager) should be able to develop universal standards, regulations and solutions that addressed your organisation's problems.

Such perspectives encouraged us to believe that the social world was finite, that work could be broken into its parts, that people had fixed personalities, that staff were self-interested, that workers required extrinsic reward and, therefore, that there were good and bad managers/workers (Seddon 2008). In particular, attribution theory suggested that people who perceived themselves to have become successful often attributed any subsequent failure and the failures of others to individual lack of effort (Kelley 1967). In management speak these people were connected to the idea of *Theory x* managers who did not trust their employees (McGregor 1960). Such people were concerned with identifying behaviour that was different to the norm and ironing it out (Kelley 1967). Some writers critiqued rigid notions of leadership, arguing that a causal, individualistic and linear concept of power resulted in blame processes in public services (e.g. where individuals were identified as causing mistakes) (Lawler and Bilson 2010). Blame approaches have permeated discussions concerning workers in the public sector. For example, the overriding concern that has underpinned calls for public sector reform has been the assumption that public service workers do not know what they are doing, do not want to change, need coercion, require control and need to be prevented (as bad people) from doing harm (Seddon 2008).

In Pentesk the top-down nature of the initiative led some staff to question why they should take on responsibility for a change process that they perceived to belong to 'the authority' or 'the managers'. Their perspective posed questions for the notion that rational-objectivist superhuman managers will always win the day and for the idea that power can/should be monopolised by any single individual (Lawler and Bilson 2010). It would have been easy for the managers who instigated the change in Pentesk to react to staff comments and blame any difficulties on them. For example, they could have related any problems that arose with implementation to uncaring/unmotivated staff. However, it was readily understood that the problems the new initiative encountered at Pentesk related more to structural issues than attitudinal issues.

For example, at the time the Pentesk initiative was being established, a study of multi-professional working in another local authority in Scotland found that professionals felt ill prepared for integrated working and admitted to a lack of knowledge/skills concerning management and leadership of integrated multi-professional services (Davis and Hughes 2005; Davis 2011). Problems occurred in Pentesk concerning issues of line management. These types of problem are not unusual in processes of multi-professional working. They have also been uncovered by studies that suggest staff at the beginning of new initiatives have to reconsider any aspirations they have to be line managed/supervised by people with similar professional backgrounds, specialist knowledge, competence and remuneration level (Anning et al. 2006; Smith 2009). Similarly, problems can occur when staff are unsure of their colleagues' objectives, the nature of their role (core/peripheral), their line management and their ability to access appropriate professional support/mentoring etc. (Tomlinson

2003; Harker et al. 2004; Anning et al. 2006; Glenny and Roaf 2008; Stone and Rixon 2008). Some staff working within new integrated children's services have had individual fears over losing their professional identity, been uncertain of their status in new structures and felt confused as to what their role or function was (Anning et al. 2006; Beattie 2007; Fitzgerald and Kay 2008; Webb and Vulliamy 2001).

In Chapter 2 (assessment) and Chapter 3 (participation) we suggested that such uncertainty left staff poorly placed to develop proactive approaches. Indeed, these chapters (in keeping with Anning et al. 2006) highlighted a range of tensions such as that staff in multi-professional services encountered leadership dilemmas (had difficulty understanding whose role it was to instigate/lead a multi-agency referral), structural problems (concerning accountability, deployment and location of decision-making), ideological differences (regarding conceptual models, professional approaches, habits) and procedural failures (concerning protocols, information sharing and communication).

 Activity

How effective are you at setting out your role in multi-professional settings? Can you clearly articulate what your aims are? Can you state what level of leadership, management/corporate experience and responsibility you have? Do you have a formal management role or are you a leader in one of the senses of the word outlined above? What problems do you encounter signing up to new initiatives? Are you motivated by visionary leaders/ideas? How open are you to change?

Management, leadership and organisational structures

In Pentesk attempts were made to develop a multi-professional structure that involved different types of responsibility. A number of writers have differentiated between strategic and operational responsibility. They have defined strategic leadership/management as involving initiative start-up, vision setting, analysis of the environment, matching resources to aims and creation of overall strategy. They have defined operational leadership as involving building the infrastructure, team or individuals and achieving tasks (Mullins 2005). There was a complex multi-professional framework in Pentesk that incorporated different levels of collaboration, hierarchy and management. This included strategic managers in the children's services planning group and operational managers/teams (tasked with delivering, producing and implementing the initiative) having devolved responsibility. For example:

- At strategic management level most but not all members of the children's services planning group moved resources around to support the Pentesk initiative and supported the planning of the development (including aims, outlines and objectives).

- Integration teams included education welfare officers, home link teachers, family support workers and assistant family support workers. The integrated teams were fully managed teams where the manager was accountable for all work (Anning et al. 2006).

- Extended team members (e.g. social workers, community learning and development workers, support for learning teachers, behaviour support teachers, educational psychologists) were part of Pentesk children and family service but had a specific line manager who was not the integration team manager.

- Link team members were managed in separate agencies and included school nurses, health visitors, speech/language therapists, community paediatricians, child and adolescent mental health workers, Sure Start workers, physiotherapists, and police and voluntary sector services.

- There was also a network association of voluntary groups, charities and religious organisations.

The integration team managers assumed corporate responsibility for managing the integrated children and family service system for their geographical area. These managers were tasked with minding the system (ensuring agreements, procedures and protocols were followed) (Glenny and Roaf 2008). The extended teams involved different professionals taking on the role of lead professional depending on the case (Anning et al. 2006). However, there were also jointly accountable teams (where corporate responsibility was delegated to team members but team members were managed by their service managers) (Anning et al. 2006). The link team members made a significant contribution to multi-professional assessment, planning and delivery and could also be characterised as a jointly accountable team) (Anning et al. 2006). The network associates involved a non-formal team of people who worked autonomously (in line management terms) of the other teams and individually with the service user but discussed provision at network meetings/local forums (Anning et al. 2006).

The speed of change at Pentesk meant that issues arose with regard to multi-professional, procedural and structural issues. For example, there was little time to develop a shared understanding of new roles, the purpose of the new service was unclear (there were conceptual/terminology issues), some agencies only had a limited opportunity to analyse, develop and voice their concerns about how the form, roles and functions of the service would develop (there were procedural difficulties) and boundaries between services had become blurred because the process was developed in a relatively quick top-down manner and in response to an opportunity to receive resources from a national 'changing children's services fund' (there were structural problems).

Not all staff understood the new management frameworks. For example, there were inter-agency problems with geographical boundaries for the new integrated teams (e.g. not all service boundaries were co-terminous), there was uncertainty around the terminology of the new services (e.g. different professionals viewed the terms 'early intervention' to mean non-crisis/low status, preventative, capacity building and/or early years services) and confusion concerning the status of the new family support worker role (it was a permanent degree-level post but some staff referred to it as an unqualified/non-professional role).

This is not unusual because it can take time for integrated teams to develop a clear understanding of new frameworks and their roles within (Anning et al. 2006). Staff/managers in Pentesk also found that a number of participants experienced difficulty overcoming their preoccupation with the traditional structures of statutory services (e.g. those related to children at risk, in care or experiencing disability) and that not all staff shared the vision of those who promoted the concept of multi-professional working (Smith 2009). It is somewhat ironic that an initiative that aimed to foster better working relationships encountered such early hurdles but we do not put this observation forward as a criticism of Pentesk because the nature of multi-professional working is that funding sources are always complex and the advocates for change in Pentesk had a one-off opportunity to receive start-up funding that was time limited which meant that they had less time than they would have hoped for to plan the initiative.

Similarly, the Pentesk initiative had to cope with existing cultures of management. Smith and Davis (2010) argued that many initiatives in children's services are often underpinned by the false assumption that professionals readily act as change agents. In Pentesk problems occurred with both staff and managers. For example, Smith (2009) found that technical rational approaches were utilised in Pentesk by some managers at a strategic level to resist change in statutory provisions and keep resources within traditional boundaries. This finding was similar to those of other writers who have argued that technical rational local authority frameworks are sometimes utilised as an excuse to ration or protect very limited resources (Hill and Tisdall 1997; McGhee and Waterhouse 2002; Jeffrey 2003).

Staff at Pentesk encountered problems because they had poorly developed starting points from which to engage in partnership working in multi-professional work (e.g. a lack of understanding of what partnership meant) (Smith and Davis 2010). Similarly, the tendency for changes to children's services in some local authorities in Scotland to occur in a top-down manner meant that managers took time to get acceptance for the shift to new forms of joined-up working. In particular (and in a similar way to other studies, e.g. Beattie 2007), staff indicated they had difficulties coping with the context the new initiative was to be placed in simply due to the sheer volume of demands being placed on them in their roles.

Top-down standardised approaches

The top-down nature of the early days of the initiative in Pentesk can be connected to technical rational management theories that advocate standardisation and regulation as ways to improve organisations (e.g. classical and strategic management) (Lawler and Bilson 2010). Managers at Pentesk concentrated on sorting out issues of structure in a top-down manner, realigning boundaries/staff and developing standardised joint assessment protocols. Ideas concerning standardisation stem from the belief that it is possible for managers and organisations to develop objective impartial, impersonal, open and transparent approaches that improve services because forms of provision are no longer decided by individuals but established through specific, systematic and imposed criteria (Dahlberg et al. 2007). Systematic rational approaches have focused on the organisation as a strategic scientific system, highlighted the generalisability/ predictability of group dynamics and promoted the need to manage out uncertainty (Lawler and Bilson 2010).

Such approaches have been described as emanating from mechanistic and militaristic metaphors and as imposing hierarchies, being logical/ methodical, involving command (one manager), requiring control, directing staff (on one track), establishing planning, developing reports, setting budgets, enforcing rules/discipline, creating impersonal relationships, paying by results and seeing service users' needs as being easy to predict (Gulick and Urwick 1937; Fayol 1949; Urwick 1952; Brech 1957; Mullins 2005; Armstrong 2009; Lawler and Bilson 2010). These ideas require you to manage the technical aspects of your organisation through hierarchical responsibility, routines, greater scientific selection/training of managers/workers, specialisation, measuring/monitoring of work performance, reduction of workers' abilities to exercise judgement and the use of scientific evaluation (Weber 1947; Taylor 1964; Harrison 2002; Lawler and Bilson 2010).

Standardisation concerned three main areas in public services: structural (e.g. group size, staff level, training, staff/service user ratios and content of service provision), procedural (e.g. behaviour of service users, relationships between service user and staff, process of service delivery and activities carried out) and outcome focused (e.g. service user development, attainment, satisfaction, etc.) (Dahlberg et al. 2007). Professionals experienced a situation where all aspects of their work became controlled by measures decided by others (e.g. inputs, outputs, targets, appraisal, quality indicators, etc.) (Cowan 1996). In many cases the development of these approaches did not involve dialogue, co-construction or interaction between those that created the quality indicators and those that used them (Dahlberg et al. 2007; Munroe 2011).

Such approaches are now referred to as 'McDonaldisation' or 'command and control approaches' because they have led to apparently efficient assembly-line type working (Ritzer 1992; Seddon 2008; Lawler and Bilson 2010). The have also been believed by some politicians to involve the best techniques for modernising the public sector (Seddon 2008). Their usefulness is associated with the hierarchical nature of activity design/management, their emphasis on economies of scale (the use of universal/standardised process of production or centralising of administration) and their preoccupation with benchmarking (standards that can be copied across organisations) (Seddon 2008; Munroe 2011).

If such technical rational approaches had been utilised in Pentesk when early problems concerning staff motivation arose, senior managers may have examined the management structures (to see who had operational responsibility for motivating the workers to engage more with the initiative), instigated blame processes (e.g. held meetings to hold managers/workers to account) or thrown money at the issues (e.g. funded overtime, promotion or new resources). Such ideas have been associated with theories of *transactional leadership* that have examined the relationship between leaders and staff and recommended that managers connect incentives such as bonuses to the need to set standards (Burns 1978; Lawler and Bilson 2010). These approaches assumed that workers required extrinsic rewards (e.g. financial gain, social opportunities or gifts) rather than intrinsic (the feeling of satisfaction gained from a job well done).

Standardisation and performance

Standardised approaches have also been associated with the idea that organisations should have corporate goals/missions and that performance should be regularly measured in public services organisations, departments and teams using specific techniques defined by catchy acronyms (e.g. SMART – specific, measurable, achievable, realistic and time-bound; SWOT – strengths, weaknesses, opportunities, threats; and MBO – management by objectives (e.g. Drucker 1974; Hill and Jones 1995; Lawler and Bilson 2010). Processes of measurement have focused on cost, apparent efficiency, resource management (how many staff to do how much work) and activity measurement (Rose 1975; Seddon 2008). Such ideas (referred to as logical positivism (Schwandt 1996; Dahlberg et al. 2007)) have enabled notions of quality and efficiency to be centralised in the form of national performance indicators, star ratings and other symbols (Dahlberg et al. 2007).

Objective notions of quality were based on the perspective that quantitative, generalised and systematic measurement criteria could be used to describe the true or essential features of a service (Dahlberg et al. 2007). Experts in public services were encouraged to develop stable, rational and permanent criteria that defined the essence of a service and that could be passed down to others to apply to their work practices (Dahlberg et al. 2007; Munroe 2011). The aim was to remove complexity and diversity in the name of quality (Dahlberg et al. 2007). In multi-professional settings such approaches have been connected to the concept of governance (individual responsibility, robustness, clarity, proceduralisation, reporting, registration, standardisation, regulation and accountability) (Simmons 2007; Lawler and Bilson 2010).

The problem with such impersonal approaches is that some of the structures they create fail to fulfil their aim of efficiency and often result in new barriers. For example, professionals use new rules to reinforce old boundaries. Command and control systems are criticised for denying the humanity of the people who participate in them, for overusing targets at the expense of goals that set the direction of travel, for taking punitive action when people fail to follow protocols, bearing down on staff who fail to meet targets, for blaming individuals for the lack of delivery and for setting up false measurements/inspection criteria (Seddon 2008; Lawler and Bilson 2010). For example, it was argued that a frontline staff member in a housing benefit office who took a call from a service user could appear to be efficient because they logged the issue and passed it on in a short space of time (thus achieving their work objectives and activity targets (Seddon 2008)). However, in reality back-office approaches created waste because the issues stacked up in the back office (were 'sifted, sorted and shunted' but not quickly resolved (Seddon 2008: 122)). Here, staff effort was wasted because workers had to request more information, the caller's issue was not resolved at the first point of contact and, in the longer term, greater resources were required to process the call (Seddon 2008 refers to this as demand failure).

Similarly, some studies found that it was unclear as to whether formalisation and centralisation in the public sector actually worked and that the utility of these approaches most likely depended on the stability of the organisational environments (Boyne 2002). Boyne (2002) concluded that the evidence from research pointed towards a contingent relationship between culture, structure, strategy, processes and performance. Similarly, other writers argued that a focus on one specific thing in an organisation was likely to boost one kind of performance at the expense of other forms (Cameron and Freeman 1991).

The use of summative performance indicators (in relation to external verification, praise and sanction) was found to be corrosive and corrupting of the indicators themselves because trust was shifted from individuals to systems (and managers had an incentive to manipulate the indicators). Advocates seemed to loose sight of the fact that an indicator is simply one measure of an activity (Glenny and Roaf 2008) that should only be utilised as a formative starting point for cautious learning, trust construction and relationship building (Freeman 2002; Jones and Leverett 2008).

We saw this type of problem in Dunlean where reticence to instigate discussions and follow protocols led to subsequent acute situations and the deployment of costly provision (emergency social work response to analyse the incident and acute child care provisions to look after children until they could be housed with their grandparents). Seddon (2008) argued that the problem with standardised approaches such as SMART is that they promote the development of arbitrary measures because people do not know what to measure. That is, proponents of such approaches assume that knowledge of what to measure is readily available. However, very often performance measures count activity (e.g. response times) rather than pulling together collective intelligence/understanding of service demand (e.g. identifying different perspectives of what people require/what their problem is), examining capability (e.g. the organisation's/worker's ability to deliver what people require), measuring achievement in service user's terms, designing against demand (from customers) and ensuring resources, experience and products flow to satisfy the demand (Seddon 2008).

Indeed, the focus on inefficiency has been criticised for at best being silly and at worst barbaric for the way it pressurises workers (Rose 1975). In the Dunlean and Pentesk case studies staff were under pressure to complete inter-agency referral assessments within a set period of time (as little as 21 days). Such approaches can put staff off from instigating procedures. In the Dunlean case no one person appeared to know that the children did not feel safe at home, that their parents were often drunk, that there was a great deal of conflict in the house and that the state of the children's living conditions was appalling. Yet they should have, hence the standardised assessment process did not work. This has led to a criticism of procedures that concentrate on the timing of assessment at the expense of ensuring assessment is carried out by professionals with sufficient knowledge and skills to help (Munroe 2011).

Some authors have tried to defend standardised approaches, suggesting, for example, that proponents such as Taylor had been misunderstood and that critics ignored attempts to use the approach to create harmony (Locke 1982; Drucker 2007). However, it is important to note that efficient processes (even where they attempt to lead to more equitable distribution of resources or greater harmony) do not necessarily fulfil the needs/wishes of service users or actually lead to helpful outcomes (for example, they can often place too much emphasis on speed of action rather than complexity/appropriateness of response (Bilson and Thorp 2007; Seddon 2008; Lawler and Bilson 2010)). This has resulted in managers and staff meeting targets rather than actually creating plans that discover, respond to and meet the requirements of the family (Lawler and Bilson 2010).

It has been argued that the problems of the public sector have stemmed from service designs being based on opinion not knowledge, targets ignoring the member of the public's perspective of the service, staff cheating/gaming the targets, managers creating a vicious circle by imposing more controls (e.g. to attempt to stop more gaming) and the imposition of quasi-market approaches (e.g. call centres) without proper evaluation (Seddon 2008).

In the early days of organisational development scientific management and mass production approaches led to workforce unhappiness, high staff turnover and the development of trade unions. For example, Ford's original assembly line approach had a worker turnover of just three months and systems theorists found that later top-down approaches such as work allocation systems tended to decrease control of work rather than increase it (Seddon 2008). It was concluded that command and control approaches actually worsen services because they sap morale, create unhappiness and prevent public services from valuing variety (Seddon 2008). In particular they are perceived to set workers/professionals against each other because they have to compete for limited resources and rewards.

Multi-professional hierarchy

Some authors have identified problems with building multi-professional relationships. For example, they have suggested that staff feel their professional identities are at risk, resent having to work with staff who do not have the same qualifications as them and/or perceive themselves to be deskilled if they have to pass on to others their skills, roles, duties, knowledge and experience (Anning 2006; UEA 2007; Stone and Rixon 2008; Walker 2008; Davis 2011). Cultural barriers related to different concepts and practices can mean that service users are assessed and treated differently because some professionals stick to their own methods of assessment and disregard new ways of thinking/working enshrined in multi-professional protocols (Davis

2011). Caring and personal service professions such as teaching, nursing, social work, community education, etc. have sometimes in the past been regarded as 'semi-professions' because their autonomy, knowledge and power has been mediated through state control (Carr-Saunders 1955; Johnson 1972; Halmos 1973).

Semi-professionals were once contrasted with 'full' traditional professions such as medicine, law and the clergy that claimed to have 'knowledge' which was held only by them, was useful to society and as such secured their place in society. Many professions have traditionally exercised 'occupational closure' and defined their own boundaries through the adoption of specific training/qualifications, self-regulation and professional hierarchies, etc. (Rugland 1993; Sims et al. 1993; MacDonald 1995; Banks 1998a, 1998b; Freeman 2002; Powell and Hewitt 2002; Aldridge and Evetts 2003; Tomlinson 2003; Frost 2005; Anning et al. 2006; Walker 2008). Writers have argued that traditional professions can be recognised by the way they have:

- guarded their knowledge carefully through 'occupational closure' (e.g. entitlement to gain knowledge traditionally came from self-regulated training programmes) (Collins 1990; Freidson 1994)

- required trainees to be inducted into a profession and to satisfy their professional colleagues that they have the ability to reflect both theoretically and critically on their practice (Carr 1999; Freidson 1994)

- provided inductees with invaluable knowledge concerning the 'officially accepted facts' of the professional/social world, the underlying principles of their profession, the ways their profession operates on a day-to-day basis and their duties as members (Freidson 1994: 44).

Such writing has been used to explain why some professionals dominate multi-professional meetings (e.g. doctors and psychologists) and why some people resist change in management/supervision structures. For example, in some local authorities there has been a great deal of conflict when it has been suggested that teachers, social workers and psychologists might be line managed by other professions (despite opportunities being provided for joint/shared management (Davis 2011)). This sort of resistance has been connected to professional discomfort concerning the public sector becoming more functional, the emergence of managerialism (the idea that managers have the right to manage, be in control and ignore the need to build consensus and take account of professional traditions) and increases in state control of professional knowledge, autonomy and power (e.g. through competence frameworks and qualifications benchmarking) (Haug 1973; Flynn 1990; MacDonald 1995; Fergusson 2000; Ozga 2000; Lawler and Bilson 2010). Writers on multi-professional working in the early years have suggested that different types of approaches can be utilised to overcome these issues, including new forms of management (e.g. profession-led, team manager, joint/shared management/supervision) and leadership (e.g. coaching/mentoring/ guiding, strategic, motivating, entrepreneurial) (Aubrey 2010).

There was less inter-professional resistance to the structural changes in Pentesk because most professionals maintained their specialist lines of supervision. However, Pentesk still encountered problems between professionals at a very basic attitudinal level because of issues of professional hierarchy. The development of multi-professional identities can be hindered by notions of professional stereotyping (Smith and Davis 2010; Walker 2008). For example, despite the fact that the Pentesk initiative put collaboration at the heart of its proposal, some professionals downplayed the role of non-traditional work roles. They appeared unaware of research that suggests most professionals will at some point work in inter-disciplinary children's service teams and the recent proliferation of a range of new multi-professional roles in children and family services (Fitzgerald and Kay 2008). For example, some staff from recent professions (such as teaching, social work and health visiting) were quite dismissive of the new family support worker roles, referring to them as paraprofessional. We can only speculate as to why some professionals would treat family support workers as inferior to themselves and refer to them as paraprofessionals. They might simply have been mimicking behaviour they had experienced themselves (e.g. their behaviour could have involved the reproduction of their own previous dismissal by traditional professions such as lawyers, psychiatrists and doctors). Alternatively it might simply have been a sign that they themselves were feeling stressed by the speed of change.

Davis (2011) connected professional hierarchy to organisational structures and argued that in the most hierarchical of settings there is greater occupational demarcations. He suggested (in keeping with other authors) that in hierarchical children and family services specific professionals were more likely to avoid activities they deemed to be lower than their level, privileged the role of statutory services, had little face-to-face contact with children/families, possessed poorly defined case loads, avoided mundane tasks and delegated their own roles to others (Davis and Hughes 2005; Fox 2005; Rowe 2005; Aubrey 2010). Similarly, it has been argued that hierarchies have led to differential treatment in terms of work/case load allocation, reluctance to share information, reluctance to develop a common language, exclusion from meetings and specific professionals avoiding face-to-face contact or home visits with children and families (Rowe 2005; Davis and Hughes 2005; Billingham and Barnes 2009; Aubrey 2010; Davis 2011). It is important to realise that hierarchy often acts as a barrier to innovation and creativity and therefore such issues need to be addressed early on when we are trying to stimulate new forms of multi-professional working (Csikszentmihalyi 1996; Ibáñez et al. 2010; Davis 2011).

It has been found that hierarchical assumptions about the superiority of traditional professions can lead to conflict between traditional and new professional groupings. This type of hierarchical conflict occurred in Dunlean where senior staff (the head teachers) did not consult specific staff (support workers in the special school and early years workers in a centre co-located with the school that Frankie had previously attended), despite the fact that these staff had more face-to-face experience working with Frankie and Jenny, understood their home situation best and knew that they were siblings.

It has been argued that the emergence of joined-up, integrated and multi-professional children and family services has created tensions for professionals (particularly in relation to the new forms of regulation and the transition to new professional identities) (Anning et al. 2006; Davis 2011). For example, some professionals are unwilling to pass information across professional boundaries (Anning et al. 2006; Jones and Leverett 2008; Walker 2008; Billingham and Barnes 2010).

In Dunlean, professional hierarchy and prejudice prevented the inclusion of non-degree professionals (Davis and Hughes 2005; Davis 2011). In contrast to these exclusionary approaches, non-degree practitioners in children's services are very clear about the professional nature of their job, and their ability to work autonomously and obtain the training/qualifications that support their professional role (e.g. in Scotland SCQF Level 7/8 qualifications such as Higher National Certificates/Higher National Diplomas (HNCs/HNDs) equivalent to first/second-year university level and EQF Level 5) (Davis and Hughes 2005; Davis 2011). For example, at

Pentesk educational welfare officers with HNDs and family support assistants with HNCs carried out initial assessment, delivered family/pupil support and discussed/reviewed/evaluated cases with children, families and other professionals.

It has been argued that any worker who has obtained such a qualification and takes on such an important role should be considered to be a fellow professional who can contribute positively to multi-professional services (Davis 2011). Indeed, some studies that have highlighted the importance of degree-level qualifications have also found significant improvement in outcomes for children related to non-degree practitioner qualifications (DfES 2004b). People who work at this level have sought to be recognised as professionals in their own right and have demonstrated the aspiration to expand their roles, take on more responsibility and be part of a career structure that enables them to achieve degree-level qualifications (e.g. in Scotland the BA in Childhood Practice) (Davis and Hughes 2005; Rowe 2005; Davis 2011).

Professional stereotyping initially led to confusion as to whether the new Pentesk initiative was a service, an approach, a process or a profession (in reality it involved all of these) (Smith and Davis 2010). For example, the integrated core teams worked in and across a range of service structures/stages/tiers including the following:

- Stage 1 involved single services being available to a child within a universal setting.

- Stage 2 included single agency support (e.g. physiotherapy, child and adolescent mental health services, behaviour support in schools, etc.).

- Stage 3 involved two or more agencies delivering multi-agency specialist support within and/or outwith the universal/community setting.

Issues arose with recruitment and retention of staff members working in family support worker roles (who came from teaching, social work, community and nursing services). Some of these staff members choose to return to posts aligned with their old professional identities (Smith and Davis 2010). However, it should be noted that the long-term rewards of changes in professional identity often outweigh short-term problems and that not all staff exhibit elitism concerning professional identities (Anning et al. 2006). Much of the integrated service delivery in Pentesk took place through locality forums and required a great deal of debate, discussion and information-sharing. In the short term, a great deal of explanation was required concerning the roles of the family support workers and the nature of the integrated, extended and link teams. However, in the longer term the forum process assisted multi-professional staff to understand, reflect and debate the change processes taking place within children's services and the family support worker role became more embedded (Smith and Davis 2010).

In Pentesk the processes of professional demarcation were also initially entwined with local politics and vested interests (e.g. regarding distribution of resources) (Smith and Davis 2010). However, it should not be assumed that any one specific professional grouping is more elitist than others or that any professional group is homogeneous (Friedson 1983; Larson 1997; Frost 2001; Anning et al. 2006; Leathard 2003a; Aubrey 2010; Smith and Davis 2010; Davis 2011). It is important here to recognise that all professionals from a specific grouping (e.g. teachers, nurses, educational psychologists, health visitors, social workers) are not the same (Davis 2011). For example, Davis and Hughes (2005) quite clearly differentiated between teachers who worked collaboratively with HNC-qualified staff and those who did not. So it should not be assumed that all teachers were prejudiced at Pentesk. Indeed, these issues arose because it took time to develop trust, people had real fears (e.g. concerning loss of status) and spaces to work out those fears (e.g. local forums) had only recently been set up.

Marketisation and professionalism

In the previous chapter (Chapter 3 on participation) we suggested that ideas of choice in the public sector had been problematic when they were used, for example, to manipulate participatory processes in ways that resulted in service outcomes being limited to a single reduced/limited set of aims (based on the service provider's own idea of what the problem was) (Seddon 2008). Marketisation ideas in the public sector attempted to redefine choice in technical rational ways and to promote the notion that workers, businesses and organisations should meet customer need (Dahlberg et al. 2007). The notion of meeting customer need was particularly welcomed by those who strove to 'empower' service users, promote equal opportunities and ensure service users experienced positive outcomes (Banks 1992; Dahlberg et al. 2007). However, the concept of empowerment has been a challenge in both the public and private sector.

In the public sector, the concept of 'empowerment' has been defined as problematic where politicians have claimed to be empowering local communities by apparently passing decision-making over the heads of public service managers (they did not trust) to local people (e.g. in local votes) but actually kept in place performance targets/ audits and financial constraints that disempowered everyone (Seddon 2008). Critiques of public sector ideas of 'empowerment' have also come from writing that has connected disability studies to multi-professional working. This writing suggests that the concept of empowerment is problematic if it perceives power to be a gift that is provided by professionals to service providers (in the sense that the gift process can be patronising). In the private sector empowerment has been used by command and control managers to disempower people (e.g. by managers who put staff on empowerment courses and then place them back in systems where they have no power) (Seddon 2008). Such approaches to empowerment are contrasted with ideas of 'self-empowerment': a state of being which people can achieve for themselves when societal barriers are removed and/or professionals act as facilitators rather than gift givers (Davis 2006; Davis 2011).

The concept of marketisation has also been defined as problematic in social services because there is sometimes a separation between those who provide, buy and use a service. That is, there can be a separation between the customer (e.g. a local authority commissioner) and the service user (e.g. a parent/child involved in a child protection process) (Lawler and Bilson 2010). Similarly, a number of writers have argued that notions of choice have cynically been utilised by politicians to echo societal discontent with public sector employees (such as teachers' and social workers' ability to block service change/improvement and protect their vested interests) (Farnham and Horton 1996). These writers suggested that the concept of marketisation was utilised by politicians to reduce the power of professions and trade unions and led to a modernisation agenda involving legislative/policy changes, public sector reform and service users (e.g. pupils, parents and patients) becoming 'consumers' in state designed 'markets' (MacDonald 1995; Hill 1997; Ozga 2000; Shore and Wright 2000; Pierson 2004). It was argued that teaching, social work, nursing, community education and further and higher education were unable to resist an 'epidemic of reform' and subsequent 'culture of performativity' (Ball 2003: 215).

However, the view that professionals were deprofessionalised by performance, appraisal and efficiency (Haug 1973; Ozga 1995) has been challenged by writers who have argued that there is no evidence that the professions have been deskilled by the marketisation agenda (Freidson 1994; MacDonald 1995). MacDonald (1995) argued that professions had not only resisted the challenges of social and technical change but had also turned it to their advantage. This led some writers to conclude that even though the marketisation agenda had influenced issues of professional autonomy it had not necessarily reduced the effectiveness of specific professions (Patrick et al. 2003). It was argued that professions such as nursing, social work, teaching, higher education, medicine, etc. were still regarded as 'professions' even if they had become more 'accountable' in relation to training, targets, outcomes, quality indicators, etc. (Patrick et al. 2003).

Similarly, a number of writers have critiqued the idea that homogenised professional groupings have ever existed. They have argued that the idea of a single professional identity is problematic because people have complex personalities and professional histories (Friedson 1983; Larson 1997; Frost 2001; Leathard 2003a; Anning et al. 2006). Indeed, it has been argued that professional groupings are actually very fluid, have to regularly respond to the financial and cultural vagaries of society, have to be open to new ways of working and need to implement specific changes very quickly (e.g. changes relating to health/safety) in order to protect their service users from harm (Bottery 1998). Such perspectives suggested that professional groupings were never static, encouraged us to consider the concept of professional groupings from a critical standpoint and persuaded us to consider professionals in relation to social context. Within this context we encourage you to avoid cultures of complaint that foster stereotyping assumptions about specific professionals (e.g. that social workers are always late, teachers only care about control/discipline or youth workers lack professionalism/just want to be the trendy friends of young people) and to be open-minded about your concepts, values and practices which may stem as much from your personal life experiences as your professional ones. Indeed, it is likely to be the case that professionals are just as diverse in their personal positions as service users.

 **Activity**

A discussion with colleagues about assumptions or prejudices you have concerning different professionals could be very illuminating. Do you recognise any of the problems outlined with regard to professionalism above (e.g. that certain people are excluded from multi-professional processes)? Can you reflect on how ideas about hierarchy influence your ability to interact in multi-professional settings (e.g. share information for joint assessment processes)? Similarly, how flexible are your processes/policies/protocols concerning multi-professional working? How do issues of governance and performance cultures influence your work?

Relational multi-professional management and leadership

Some writers have contrasted hierarchical ideas of leadership and management to more interactive approaches. For example, they have highlighted approaches that have: encouraged participation (democratic leaders), supported workers to achieve (enabling leaders) and asked people to work towards a better good (transformational leaders) (Bolden et al. 2003; Armstrong 2009; Lawler and Bilson 2010).

These approaches were considered to be different to authoritarian and hierarchical approaches because they required you as a leader to be sensitive to the feelings of employees, be capable of building relationships, be able to self-assess, be politically aware, demonstrate social skills, show emotional intelligence and utilise interpersonal awareness (Schlundt and McFall 1985; Goleman 1996; Alimo-Metcalf et al. 2000; Northouse 2007; Lawler and Bilson 2010). These approaches sought to balance approaches of top-down management with participatory ideas. For example, the balanced score card approach involved managers communicating their visions to workers and subgroups, agreeing drivers/targets for success and measuring against those criteria in order to identify the critical success factors in terms of financial performance, customer service improvements, internal business processes and innovation/learning (Lawler and Bilson 2010). This approach claimed to empower staff by balancing external measures (e.g. customers' experience) and internal measures with a range of long/short-term indicators, including leading (desired outcomes), lagging (actual outcomes), subjective (worker/customer outcomes) and objective (financial outcomes) measures (Lawler and Bilson 2010). However, in the main such approaches focused on top-down management (Seddon 2008; Lawler and Bilson 2010) or the assumption that at least the manager could manage him/herself more effectively and therefore manage by example (Drucker 2007).

In contrast, we would like to encourage you to move from hierarchical notions of group leadership to viewing leadership as involving complex contingent relationships and as involving multi-wave distributive power exchange. Here, leadership is viewed as something that can be fluid, integrative and collective. This perspective invites you to be critical of writers who have promoted simplistic approaches concerning the authoritative role of the manager, suggested your role as a manager should not simply be to process/analyse information in order to work out the best way to resolve an issue, and/or asked you as a leader to utilise rationality, objectiveness and detachment (Lawler and Bilson 2010).

Some management approaches ask you to view workers as self-motivated. They have been associated with the terms *Theory Y* managers who were identified as promoting staff participation/empowerment because they perceived/wanted workers to enjoy their work (McGregor 1960) and *Theory W* managers (Shiba 1998) who were identified as trying to balance staff needs concerning security, predictability, continuity and creativity because they saw the benefits of involving staff in organisational improvement (Shiba 1998; Bolden et al. 2003; Seddon 2008; Lawler and Bilson 2010). Such writers have highlighted the need to understand the complex nature of worker motivation including their need for continuity, creativity, achievement, power and relationships (McClelland 1961; McCoy 1992; Petri 1996).

This raised issues for the formation of teams in Pentesk. For example, it has been argued that simply bringing together and calling a collection of differing professionals a 'team' does not guarantee shared knowledge is readily exchanged, integrated inter-professional working flourishes, there is seamless delivery of services or that vested interests will be overcome (Anning et al. 2006; Smith 2009; Smith and Davis 2010). When teams are brought together relationships have to be built that result in some form of conceptual unity that values the diversity of the experiences of the professionals involved (Cohen et al. 2004; Anning et al. 2006; Scott 2006; Davis 2011).

Humanistic approaches

Humanistic and human relational approaches to management and leadership emerged that valued human feelings such as intuition, promoted the notion of collective vision and involved people crafting a process in ways that drew from personal experience, harmony and intimacy with a field (Mintzberg 1987; Lawler and Bilson 2010). Human relational approaches raise important questions for you in your work concerning the politics of multi-professionalism, how multi-professionalism is negotiated in practice and how multi-professionalism and interpersonal complexity is allowed space in the workplace (Jones and Leverett 2008; Smith and Davis 2010). In particular they led to the idea that leadership should be concerned with philosophy, culture and consensus (now referred to as Theory Z and associated with Ouchi (1981)).

These ideas led to the suggestion that multi-professional initiatives required a range of processes to enable professionals from different backgrounds with different identities to break down professional barriers. These include joint training, joint problem-solving, shared goals, regular meetings, enabling spaces for dialogue, trust-building initiatives, strong/clear management, anti-discriminatory practice, etc. (Bertram et al. 2002; Gilbert and Bainbridge 2003; Leathard 2003b; Tomlinson 2003; Harker et al. 2004; Frost 2005; Milne 2005; Anning et al. 2006; Scott 2006; Fitzgerald and Kay 2008; Glenny and Roaf 2008; Stone and Rixon 2008; Walker 2008). In particular professionals were encouraged to reflect on different perspectives that underpinned their practice in order to create a counterbalance to the instrumental rationality that had featured so heavily in standardised approaches to public sector reform (Lawler and Bilson 2010).

In Chapters 2 and 3 we saw the need for such processes, e.g. to overcome deficit models in assessment processes and to establish understandings/agreements concerning different collaborative, facilitated and autonomous processes of participation. In particular these chapters highlighted the need for service providers to recognise the diverse outcomes that service providers might require (redistribution, rights, compensation, recognition, etc.).

Humanistic approaches drew their metaphors from biology (Morgan 1986; Lawler and Bilson 2010). They suggested that organisations were developing, organic, living and growing systems that required:

- staff, customer and sector involvement in strategic development

- effective recruitment, induction and appraisal

- human resource practice to be connected to business strategy

- performance to be connected to worker need, commitment, motivation and development.

> (Mayo 1945; Maslow 1954; Miller and Rice 1967;
> Lyus 1998; Mullins 2005; Lawler and Bilson 2010)

This included the idea that because an organisation was part of wider social, technical and environmental systems decision-making should be contingent on the situation (promoted by socio-technical systems theory Trist 1951, and human resource management theory MacGregor 1960). This theory was built on the presumption that an organisation was only as good as the people who worked within it, staff were the organisation's greatest assets and the perception that organisational efficiency came from evidence-informed/based practice that included processes of learning/questioning that enabled adaptation, change and modification (Trist and Bamforth 1951; Etzioni 1964; Schön 1978; Senge 1990; Dodgson 1993; Legge 2005; Mullins 2005; Visser 2007; Lawler and Bilson 2010).

Here, the manager was perceived to be a team leader who involved others in decision-making processes, worked out the things that motivated staff and helped them to direct their performance (Mintzberg 1987; Mullins 2005). A number of authors connected humanistic approaches to the concept of worker commitment. They argued that workers gave substantial effort if they were committed to the organisation (held its values/goals), could participate in decision-making and could be encouraged to see that their own beliefs, acts and interests are commensurate with those of the organisations (Etzioni 1964; Porter et al. 1974; Salancik and Pfeffer 1977; Armstrong 2009).

These processes take time to embed and they were therefore missing in the early days of the Pentesk initiative. Moreover, some human relation approaches such as Maslow's (1954) hierarchy of physiological, safety, intimacy, esteem and self-actualisation needs overemphasised the individual characteristics of staff and the two-way nature of leader/manager roles at the expense of recognising collective notions of leadership (Lawler and Bilson 2010). A further criticism of humanistic approaches was that processes of participation were often employed as a manipulative ploy of the manager/organisation (in a similar way to tokenistic choice processes discussed in Chapter 3 and marketisation forms of participation discussed above in this chapter). For example, Lawler and Bilson (2010) pointed out that despite being concerned with living systems, rewarding workers and learning 'cultures' these approaches still emphasised the efficiency and survival aspects of other technical rational theories of management. Indeed, a number of authors have indicated that humanistic approaches had several drawbacks, including the fact that they failed to balance their humanistic principles with their technical need for managerialist design, continued to place leadership responsibility in the hands of the few, insisted that a single homogeneous organisational culture was achievable/desirable, still set the agenda of the organisation from the top and lacked the ability to quickly adapt to changing, messy or turbulent circumstances (Schein 1999; Land 2000; Bilson and Thorpe 2007; Lawler and Bilson 2010). The next chapter will examine how the Pentesk initiative took account of humanistic issues over the longer term and tried to move to more dialogic (discursive) approaches that valued different perspectives.

 Activity

Can you consider with colleagues issues that create barriers to multi-professional working in your own service? Can you create a table from the following headings (developed from Mullins 2005) and write examples of issues that have influenced management and leadership of change in places you have worked?

- History, Function, Size, Local, Routine, Ritual, Lore, Symbols
- Internal/External Control, Policy, Power, Funding and Structure
- Participation, Unfairness and Inequity
- Trust, Dialogue, Identity and Loyalty
- Departmentalisation, Specialisation, Informal and Formal Territory
- Group, Individual/Personal, Departmental, Organisational, Generational Goals

Conclusion

This chapter drew on a case study of a Scottish local authority to demonstrate the complex nature of change in children's services and to encourage you to move away from hierarchical approaches. The problems of the Pentesk initiative were connected to an over-reliance on the concept of visionary leaders and change agents, a multi-professional hierarchy that downplayed the status of new staff roles, top-down standardised approaches (including performance indicators) and difficulties with integrating new frameworks into existing practices/contexts. The chapter contrasted rigid approaches in organisations with humanistic and relational approaches that suggested that multi-professional working might benefit from more interactive leadership roles. This issue is investigated in more depth in the next chapter in relation to spaces for dialogue that were developed in Pentesk to facilitate more collaborative, joint and interactive multi-professional approaches.

Recommended further reading

Dahlberg, G., Moss, P. and Pence, A. (2007) *Beyond Quality in Early Childhood Education and Care: Languages of Evaluation*, 2nd edn. London: Falmer Press.

Leathard, A. (2003) 'Models for interprofessional collaboration', in A. Leathard (ed.) *Interprofessional Collaboration: From Policy to Practice in Health and Social Care*. Hove: Brunner-Routledge.

Walker, G. (2008) *Working Together for Children: A Critical Introduction to Multi-Agency Working*. London: Continuum.

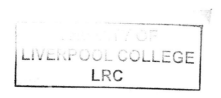

5

Contemporary approaches to multi-professional leadership and management

Chapter Overview

The previous chapter, when discussing innovation in Pentesk local authority, highlighted the tension between hierarchical and relational ideas of leadership and management and concluded that some human relational approaches failed to move beyond individualised ideas concerning staff and managers. Similarly, Chapter 2 (assessment, planning and delivery) argued that joint assessment required more systematic approaches to emerge in local authorities. This chapter revisits the Pentesk case study a number of years on in the process to examine what a systemic approach looks like and to illustrate the contemporary ideas, conceptual frames, collaborative structures and complex relationships that could provide a flexible framework for systemic multi-professional working. It concludes that there are benefits from viewing reflexivity as both an individual and collective approach, that reflective plural approaches that do so can have value in any organisation (whether in crisis, change or static) and that such approaches are particularly useful in settings that involve more than one organisation and management structure.

Case Study

This chapter continues to analyse the Pentesk case study in order to consider contemporary leadership and management issues in integrated children's services. In the last chapter we discussed the hierarchical structure in Pentesk. This chapter contrasts this top-down structural context with attempts in Pentesk to promote joint working through approaches of shared responsibility and collaborative dialogue. It specifically discusses the role of multi-professional teams and forums. The teams and forums were set up to enable discussion concerning community and service development, coordination of needs assessment, inclusive access to universal services, the provision of a range of in-school and out-of-school support, the provision of family support across localities, flexible services for children who require targeted intervention and the joint commissioning of services that were responsive to local need.

Reflexive managers, leaders and individuals

Reflexivity is a complex concept. In its simplest form it requires thought and change. It differs from the concept of reflection that only requires thought rather than change. It has been argued in anthropology and sociology that reflexivity enables individuals to become aware of their own prejudices and compare them to the life views of the people they are working with (Wax 1971; Phillipson 1972; Okely 1975; Rabinow 1977; Holy 1984).

It has been argued that reflexive practice is an essential part of the work of the professional (Schön 1987; Brookfield 1995). The ability to stand back, review and be critical of the 'real world' allows the professional to challenge power relations and the production/reproduction of knowledge. In Pentesk the integrated team manager role involved reflexive leadership. It was built on the assumption that such individuals should support emergent processes, encourage worker autonomy and promote staff interconnections (Lawler and Bilson 2010). This type of role utilises the individual manager's ability to be a sense-maker who reflects on and embraces diversity, avoids privileging one perspective over another and recognises the expertise of others while still remaining part of a hierarchy (Lawler and Bilson 2010).

Reflexive practice has been identified as a key aspect of professionalism during the development of standards/benchmarks that underpin the variety of qualifications that professionals achieve prior to entering multi-professional children and family services (Collins 2008; Davis 2011). A key aspect of reflexive practice involves practitioners learning and improving their practice through a process of reviewing their experiences within the workplace.

Davis (2011) concluded (in keeping with Moss and Petrie 2002) that we need to recognise integrated services as socially dynamic spaces and that practitioners should be encouraged to constantly question their thoughts, practices and relationships. This perspective is built on the premise that multi-professional working is different to processes where scientists carry out independent laboratory observations/experiments. Indeed, multi-professional working does not occur in such vacuums. When we worked in multi-professional settings similar to the Pentesk forums, we noticed that different professionals were already oriented to a set of meanings that were bound up in their professional and personal lives, that service users had different lives to us and that we could not assume that children and parents interpreted their life events in the same way that we did (Davis 1996, 1998; Davis et al. 2001).

Multi-professional working requires professionals to create time to speak to individuals, reflect on their own positions and develop an instinct for moments that require self-awareness, for example when a child suddenly becomes uncommunicative, a pupil turns up at school in an unkempt manner or a group meeting goes very quiet after we have said something (Davis et al. 2001). A number of writers suggest that it is not possible to have a 'clean slate' approach to our perspectives, that the professional observer's own perspectives are ever present and that we must therefore acknowledge our views and put them to creative use (Okely 1975; Agar 1996; Davis 1996, 1998). That is, it is professional to use the differences between our own and other people's perspectives in meetings as points for discussion and it is unprofessional to hide/hold back any reactions, interpretations that are pertinent to the decision-making process (Davis 2011).

In relation to the forums we encourage you to recognise that each group will involve different characters with different backgrounds and contrasting people will be more or less active (Bolton 2010). Bolton (2010) has recommended six principles of group work responsibility, suggesting that each member is responsible for:

- their own ethical behaviour

- a willingness to trust enough to start the process

- self-respect, beliefs, actions, feelings and values

- generosity and the spirit of give and take

- positive regard, confidence, confidentiality and respect

- valuing of diversity and reflecting on, sharing and understanding the politics of difference.

(Bolton 2010)

It is recommended that ground rules are established, e.g. concerning group boundaries, respect and function, and that group members consider issues of timing, size, equipment, attendance, funding, location, contribution and listening (Bolton 2010).

Groups tend to have different stages, for example meeting new people, giving commitment, emerging conflict, conflict resolution, collective mission and end/mourning (Bolton 2010). It is important that participants are encouraged to be critically reflexive and focus on discussing issues concerning such stages rather than burying them (Davis 2011).

Some writers have encouraged professionals to use reflexivity to set aside their prejudices (Phillipson 1972). However, it is our position that, rather than setting aside your views, as far as possible you should make obvious your perspectives during team meetings, outreach visits, local forums and one-to-one discussions. Our view is built on literature that has encouraged us to think about children's services as spaces involving processes of dialogue (rather than as one-off events Moss and Petrie 2002).

A number of authors have argued that it is important that informal and formal structures are available for professionals to stimulate discussions and to agree processes of assessment, support, planning and delivery (Moss and Petrie 2002). In particular, it was argued that we needed to move from workers having a vague idea of what their job was to specifically agreeing with service users what the aims of workers' roles were and evaluating workers' practice in terms of how they met those agreed aims (Dolan 2006b). It has been argued that the starting point for reflexive practice needs to be clear discussions concerning the characteristics of the work that practitioners are involved in (Pinkerton 2006).

Workers in multi-professional settings will encounter a range of concepts that come from different subject areas, e.g. health, psychology, social care, early years, play/leisure, youth/community, criminology, childhood theory, family studies, counselling, management theory, housing, etc. Such diversity will often lead to differences in opinion; however, it is possible to utilise such moments as opportunities for analysis that develop new insights into potential ways of working, our colleagues' ways of thinking or the problems that service users are encountering (Davis 1996). The differences between your ideas and the concepts of other people should be explored to develop more precise and in-depth information on what works for different people in practice, what needs changing and what needs to be dropped. The analysis of difference has been highlighted as an important aspect of contemporary society. We are constantly required to make ourselves aware of our own prejudices and it is only by recognising the 'reflexive' nature of our everyday relationships that we can gain more considered insights into our and other people's lives (Rabinow 1977; Rorty 1980). In this way reflexive practice is thought to assist practitioners to be clear about the purpose of their role and the boundary issues they face. However, despite the apparent benefits of reflexive practice it can be confusing and difficult for professionals to do (Dolan 2006b). For all of us involved in the day-to-day practice of supporting children and families, one of the most difficult aspects of reflexive practice is actually building it into our work patterns in ways that makes sense. Many authors have suggested that the difficulties of contemporary professionals within multi-professional settings can be overcome if their systems are built on 'harmonious relationships', trust and multi-professional respect (Bertram et al. 2002; Leathard 2003b; Tomlinson 2003; Harker et al. 2004; Frost 2005; Anning et al. 2006; Stone and Rixon 2008; Walker 2008; Davis 2011).

The Pentesk initiative built better relationships on the principle that change can be stimulated by equitable rewards, relations, policies and practices and cooperation can be based on openness, a willingness to resolve conflict and high-quality career design, development and evolution (Mullins 2005). A great deal of effort was expended in Pentesk in the attempt to follow the recommendation that they should develop improved processes of communication and greater multi-professional trust (Bertram et al. 2002; Leathard 2003b; Harker et al. 2004; Frost 2005; Anning et al. 2006; Stone and Rixon 2008).

It has been argued that strong relationships should be built around a core group of staff and that leaders have to ensure agreements are kept, solutions are followed through and in a sense they keep people focused on the history and aims of the system (Tomlinson 2003; Anning et al. 2006; Glenny and Roaf 2008). The forums at Pentesk enabled members of the integrated, extended and link teams (see Chapter 4 for an outline of professionals who were attached to these groups) to discuss referrals, agree/negotiate issues of lead professional responsibility and to act as catalysts/campaigners for early integrated services (through lead and example). The forums were developed to ease access to information, foster avenues of communication and enable discussion/resolution of complex issues.

Many writers have highlighted the need for discussion and dialogue in multi-professional settings. They have suggested that strong avenues of communication are required (e.g. local networks, forums and processes) to enable professional differences, discordance and conflict to be worked out (Davis 1998, 2011; Moss and Petrie 2002; Anning et al. 2006; Glenny and Roaf 2008). It is suggested that when services possess a culture of reflexivity, workers tend to be more astute service users (e.g. young people) are safer and positive outcomes are more likely to occur (Dolan 2006b). These ideas underpinned the Pentesk development. The integrated team managers were tasked with enshrining joint aims, plans and objectives, negotiating issues of workload, developing shared approaches, ensuring plans led to action and encouraging staff to follow processes, protocols and agreements. This responsibility was shared with named professionals in universal services and lead professionals from the extended and link teams and was devolved as and when needed to specific members of the various teams. The sharing of responsibility required workers to consider their different concepts regarding children and families.

Chapter 2 discussed the problems that arise when multi-professional working involves conceptual uncertainty. It highlighted a need to shift to holistic politically nuanced strengths-based working. Some workers in children's services (particularly in early years) consider themselves to be pedagogues who are able to reflexively analyse their practice, view the child as located within wider systems, work with the whole child body/mind/emotions, work with children through creative mediums and involve children and parents in processes of planning and change (Smith et al. 2000; Moss and Petrie 2002; Cohen et al. 2004; Bruce 2004; Moss and Bennett 2006; Foley 2008; Glenny and Roaf 2008; David et al. 2010). They have recognised the importance of community relationships, understood the potential for their work to involve the exploration of diversity and reflexively considered the cultural/historical context of children's lives (Smith et al. 2000; Moss and Petrie 2002; Cohen et al. 2004; Bruce 2004; Moss and Bennett 2006; Foley 2008; Glenny and Roaf 2008; David 2010). Such a shift to holistic thinking was required of staff at Pentesk.

Chapter 2 suggested that assessment processes needed to be based on joined-up approaches that were underpinned by precise referral, recording, information-sharing, assessment, management, planning, delivery, monitoring and evaluation (Walker 2008). Indeed, we feel it is very important to ensure that local frameworks for logging information, developing plans and recording agreements concerning service delivery can be reviewed/evaluated. Processes of dialogue need to be recorded in ways that are meaningful to the actors present and it is crucial that there are multi-professional processes/protocols that enable respectful exchange of information (Anning et al. 2006; Walker 2008). However, we also want to point out that written approaches can also be used in more flexible and collective ways to help professionals examine the processes, preconceptions and beliefs that subtly underpin their work. Note-taking can be a very important means of self and joint exploration (Bolton 2010). It can involve recording personal reactions, moments of interaction and everyday dilemmas as they occur (Okely 1975).

Some writers have encouraged us to develop learning journals, logs and diaries to enquire into particular events/occasions. They have suggested that practitioners should analyse what they and others did, thought, felt, believed and were prejudiced about (Bolton 2010). Practitioners have been encouraged to try out different forms of writing (poems, stories, musings, self-dialogues, visualisation, mind maps and fictional dialogues) to work through their thinking (Bolton 2010). However, deeply reflexive writing does not come easy within the busy processes of multi-professional working and it can be difficult because of the politics of the situation (Bolton 2010).

At Pentesk the integration team managers became adapt at monitoring the paperwork around cases, and over time they developed an in-depth understanding of the types of referrals that they received, the responses that children and families wanted to see and the difference between appropriate and inappropriate types of referral. They also employed the forums as places where they could discuss their experiences with staff from the locations that were developing the referrals. This enabled the sharing of knowledge on how to assess and support children and families earlier in universal services to avoid their cases becoming acute. In this sense early intervention involved a process where knowledge and skills on what families felt worked for them became more clearly articulated, shared and utilised. The development of clearer understandings has been seen as a key aspect of multi-professional working and is perceived to offer greater possibilities for innovative joint action (Aubrey 2010).

Such reflexive processes can be contrasted to the managerial worlds discussed in the previous chapter that emphasised top-down command and control approaches, that restricted the voice of professional workers, that stressed the need for operational effectiveness and that promoted the use of star ratings or similar performance measurements (Harris 2003; Seddon 2008; Lawler and Bilson 2010). Rather than concentrating on technical rational approaches the forums attempted to promote diversity, complexity and change.

Over time, managers were able to utilise the forums to support the development of worker autonomy, devolved management and more pluralist approaches. In this way they were able to soften the edges of the initial standardised and top-down nature of the Pentesk initiative. At the beginning of the process issues of power, politics and professional demarcation within the Children's Services Planning Group (CSPG) hindered the wide-ranging dissemination of information concerning the new initiative to key stakeholders. In particular conflict arose between professionals who held a 'child protection' perspective (focusing on investigative approaches and performance indicators) and those who held more contemporary ideas concerning multidisciplinary working (focusing on preventative, developmental and integrative roles). One service in particular would only engage with the integrated agenda in relation to their statutory obligations and was not interested in the strengths-based approach, early intervention or conceptual unity. Certain managers removed themselves from discursive spaces (the forums and planning groups where joint problem-solving occurred e.g. budget sharing, releasing staff for training, promoting shared values) and did not share power in the system (e.g. not attending meetings, delaying decision-making, undermining the status of locality forums). This (in keeping with Carpenter 1997; Leathard 1997; Munroe 2011) meant that traditional management methods and a bias towards reactive child protection procedures initially prevented a move from reactive to proactive welfare approaches (e.g. early intervention family support services).

For example, it was noted that one specific voluntary organisation that provided counselling services was gaining good results at a lower cost than other providers and was using approaches that enabled greater engagement with service users. Contracts were developed with this voluntary organisation that enabled an expansion of their service. This reduced costs in the longer term because the voluntary organisations' approach prevented cases from becoming acute and avoided service users having to access expensive provision.

The forums were able to overcome the early problems of the initiative by stimulating discussions concerning what a healthy organisational climate would look like, enabling greater synergy of worker, manager and organisational goals (e.g. in respect to clarifying ideas and processes of joint assessment and early intervention), and implementing processes of real and sustained worker participation, exchange and dialogue (concerning the appropriateness of specific services).

The flexible nature of the forums can be connected to writing that is critical of universal approaches and beliefs that no one perspective should be privileged over another. Such writing has called for a move away from technical rational approaches and for children and family services to enable more reflexive approaches that acknowledge a wider range of perspectives on individual action, perceive the individual to be unique, constantly developing and unpredictable, welcome dynamic, uncertain and innovative organisational relationships, challenge the idea that leadership is an entity in its own right reducible to specific technical rational characteristics, and recognise that leadership means different things in different contexts (Lawler and Bilson 2010).

These perspectives have been valuable at the individual level because they have encouraged us to understand local contexts, to think about leadership as a variable thing, to recognise that local leadership can be developed from local consensual agreements (rather than top-down patronage or reciprocal appointment) and to recognise the importance of dialogue, language and communication (Lawler and Bilson 2010). Such approaches define effective leadership as a subjective concept that is dependent on the different views of the people experiencing your leadership. It also associates leadership with hindsight, context, story/narrative and collective sense-making (Muldoon 2004; Weick et al. 2005; Lawler and Bilson 2010).

Collective reflexivity, dialogue and sense-making

Dialogue was highlighted as important in multi-professional processes as it is the main way to gain access to people's subjective views, co-construct shared meanings, create common purpose, clarify knowledge, create opportunities for thinking and establish understandings (Cooper 2002; Moss and Petrie 2002; Lawler and Bilson 2010). The workers at Pentesk would not necessarily have perceived themselves to be involved in narrative story-telling and structured conversations. However, the forums could be defined as such because they were utilised as a structure that enabled processes for understanding organisational life, a place to recognise past achievements, a location to build significant relationships, a setting that provided opportunities to develop new insights and a site for generating creative plans (Ochberg 1994; Ford and Lawler 2007; Lawler and Bilson 2010).

On an individual level reflexive leadership has been associated with self-awareness, regulation, balance and transparency (Mazutis and Slawinski 2008; Lawler and Bilson 2010). Such approaches have incorporated ideas related to process/maintenance such as active listening, empathetic listening, therapeutic listening, participation, critical reflection, shared conflict resolution and trust (Mayo 1945; Wolvin and Coakley 1993; Stewart and Cash 2000; Halone and Pecchioni 2001; Hargie and Dickson 2006; Lawler and Bilson 2010). They have also involved task-related functions such as evaluation, coordination, direction setting, instigation and energising (Lawler and Bilson 2010). Such approaches when working well enable a more community-based and networked approach to be taken to organisational development that disperses leadership, draws from multiple sources and enables the direction of the organisation to be developed collaboratively (Lawler and Bilson 2010).

Such collaboration requires multi-professional working to be conceived as a long-term process. For example, a key aspect of the initiative at Pentesk was that it was embedded into existing (though adapted) structures. Of particular importance was the fact that the professionals in the new integrated teams were given permanent contracts and experienced similar working conditions to other professionals in the forums (though not exactly the same conditions as professionals from agencies such as health, police, etc. which were not part of the local authority structures). In the previous chapter we demonstrated that the technical rational structures in Pentesk caused some barriers for the initiative (e.g. in relation to professional hierarchy). It is important to note that over the longer term the forums demonstrated it was possible for issues of professional hierarchy to be overcome. For example, the integrated teams were not on time-limited contracts and the range of professionals involved recognised/agreed this was an initiative that was not going to go away and therefore concentrated on working through its teething problems.

The Pentesk initiative can be connected to literature that suggests innovation and change occurs when organisations show recognition/respect for the contributions of diverse professional identities, groups and agencies. At the centre of this perspective is the idea that pluralist approaches respect diversity and try to learn from difference where as technical rational perspectives attempt to reduce cultural relations to that which is co-joined, common or similar and therefore try to coalesce, assimilate and iron out diversity (Rorty 1980). It took time in Pentesk for the integrated, extended and link teams to move to a stage beyond mere collaboration where professionals fully understood their differences. Some writers have argued that the shift to more integrated approaches requires the development of a common identity, philosophy and goals (Fitzgerald and Kay 2008; Foley and Rixon 2008). We think it is important to unpack this idea and rephrase it to suggest that it is important that there are shared structures, processes and understandings but that these do not need people to completely give up their identities and differences.

In earlier chapters we have criticised deficit model approaches that do not value the diversity of childhood and overemphasise the need for approaches that intervene in children's lives in order to make them more like their peer group. In a similar way (drawing from the work of Seddon 2008 and Lawler and Bilson 2010) we would like to encourage you to adopt approaches that value your colleagues diversity and encourage you as a worker, leader or manager to help to create work spaces that value the variety of identities that different workers, children, families and communities possess.

Such approaches can be connected to poststructural and postmodern writing on multi-professional children's services that has raised questions regarding issues of power/politics, hierarchy, participation and authority/truth. These approaches have called for service providers to develop a greater understanding of multiple, local, diverse (and sometimes contradictory) knowledge (Davis 2011). This writing has argued that by recognising the human frailties of professionals we can begin to develop more effective services that honestly engage with our own imperfections (Davis 2011).

The development of forums in Pentesk is commensurate with ideas in the literature on family that replace individualised notions of reflexivity (that had been critiqued for resulting in navel gazing) with interrelational notions of reflexivity that see reflexivity as being part of wider processes of social networking within organisations/services (Dolan 2006b, Pinkerton 2006). It has been argued that when different professionals in a multi-professional service build an appreciative system the service becomes effective (Glenny and Roaf 2008). An appreciative system is defined as one where issues are communicated across the system between different professionals, communication is nested (e.g. issues on the ground are fed back into local authority decision-making), local forums enable reflective collaborative practice, different professionals are able to shape the development of the service in response to local ideas, local services act as a recognised unit with which workers can identify and children/families view the service as a continuum (Glenny and Roaf 2008).

Proponents of such thinking have argued that reflexivity can help to free up professional action and enable professionals to respond to the political dogma that arises from ideas of performance, standardisation and marketisation (Lawler and Bilson 2010, Penna and O'Brien 1996). This writing draws from disciplines such as anthropology and sociology to encourage us to analyse the politics of multi-professionalism (Wax 1971; Phillipson 1972; Okely 1975; Rabinow 1977; Holy 1984; Jones and Leverett 2008; Smith and Davis 2010).

Politics exist around the concept of professional expertise. In Chapter 3 (participation) we argued that multi-professional working involved different forms of expertise and that children, families, professionals and community members should all be assumed to have some form of expertise they can draw on during participatory processes. This redefinition of the term expert requires you as a professional to be humble about your knowledge, concepts and practices, to be willing to be open to new ways of thinking and to be able to adapt to the different contexts of your work (Davis 2011). Such approaches recognise the limitations of those that make claims based on truth and authority (Corker and Shakespeare 2001).

They encourage us to include service users in processes where we discuss the concepts that underpin our work, respect their capabilities, value/validate their contribution and develop shared ownership of multi-professional process (Beresford 1999). Such shifts in power recognise the value of concepts of ambiguity, fluidity and contested truth (Parton 2000; Davis 2011). They also require us to recognise that all practice is connected to some aspect of theory, that the complex social world means no theory works all of the time and that avenues/forums of dialogue are required to enable us to continually discuss why services are not working and to rework our concepts based on shared analysis of the problems (rather than on hanging on dogmatically to dated ideas in ways that lead to oppressive services).

This way of thinking suggests that whether you are a service user, professional, community member, leader, manager, practitioner or learner you can always be a leader that takes responsibility for listening to, understanding and analysing. It encourages you as a professional involved in collective leadership to see that you are capable of promoting change/development whatever your role in your organisation and that it is possible (in keeping with Chapter 2 on assessment and Chapter 3 on participation) to support others (children, parents, staff, etc.) to take leadership roles. Our ideas are supported by writing that encourages multi-professional working to celebrate the emotional nature of public service delivery and to engage with the uncertainty, unpredictability and plurality of organisational dynamics (Lawler and Bilson 2010).

 Activity

What approaches do you use for recording personal reactions, the views of your colleagues and everyday dilemmas? Do you understand the theory, policy and practice that underpins your work? Are you able to explain your concepts clearly to colleagues and service users so that they can be involved in joint decision-making? Can you think of an example where you have noticed a difference between your own perspective and that of others (professionals, children or parents)?

Systemic multi-professional joint working

Multi-professional working requires us to look beyond the boundaries, capacities or responsibilities of a single agency (Bruner 2006). The previous chapter indicated that more consideration needs to be given to the context of the Pentesk initiative. The shift to multi-professional working occurred at a time when the local authority was experiencing a range of changes related to the localised involvement of service users in planning, the emergence of single-issue politics in response to cuts in local transport, health and welfare services, and the emergence of new forms of exclusion, e.g. from information technology. It has been argued that such factors put pressure on professionals in public services (Lawler and Bilson 2010; O'Brien and Penna 1998; Penna and O'Brien 1996).

Multi-professional practice can be interdependent, locally variable, full of conflict, ambiguous, emotional and compassionate (Lawler and Bilson 2010). In Pentesk, there was much ambiguity over the term 'integrated services' and what it implied for multi-professional working. Some writers have referred to the 'terminological quagmire' of service integration (Leathard 2003a: 5). Others have argued that there is no clarity around the meaning of integration, what it involves, the activities that define it and the professional exigencies/relationships implied by it (Scott 2006: 9). Indeed, many policy developments in this field have been criticised for not giving a clear explanation of what is meant by the term 'integrated' (Graham and Machin 2009). Professionals have been confused by the term and have been unsure where their service fits within integrated models (Graham and Machin 2009: 35).

It is important for you to realise that the reason it is difficult to define integrated working is because there is no single way to do it. It is possible to set out a rough continuum of practice related to the structures of integrated working. At the heart of the continuum is the idea that integrated working involves something more connected, joined-up, synthesised or thought through (Davis 2011). A number of authors separate out the types of integrated working into *cooperation* (smoother information sharing), *collaboration* (joint working with a service user or in a joint assessment forum), *coordination* (sharing goals/aims) and *merger* (greater synthesis of boundaries, budgets and locations) (Leathard 2003a, 2003b; Bertram et al. 2002; Cohen et al. 2004; Frost 2005; Stone and Rixon 2008; Walker 2008; Davis 2011). Within this continuum integrated working can be informal/formal, involve one or more disciplines/agencies/professions and involve working across (transagency), between (intragency) or in a shared way (interagency) (Wilson and Pirie 2000; Lloyd et al. 2001; Christie and Menmuir 2005; Scott 2006; Malin and Morrow 2007; Fitzgerald and Kay 2008).

There is a significant difference between attempts at better cooperation where services/professionals maintain their independence, approaches that strive to develop jointly planned collaboration and the most innovative change that aims to enable greater, more systematic or deliberate coordination of provision, i.e. that crosses service boundaries, involves shared planning of resources and questions the local politics of service provision (Huxham and Macdonald 1992; Leathard 2003a, 2003b; Tomlinson 2003; Frost 2005; Glenny and Roaf 2008; Stone and Rixon 2008; Fitzgerald and Kay 2008; Walker 2008; Davis 2011). Davis (2011) has suggested that the fullest form of integration (that which lies at the farthest end of the continuum) involves *processed-based service merger.* This form of integration is characterised by the amalgamation of services, synthesis, changes in professional identity, co-location, multiple site integration, budget pooling and unification (Bertram et al. 2002; Gilbert and Bainbridge 2003; Leathard 2003b; Cohen et al. 2004; Frost 2005; Scott 2006; Stone and Rixon 2008; Walker 2008).

Pentesk incorporated many of the aspects of fuller integration (e.g. there were a number of sites of co-location where a range of services were available more locally for service users). Pentesk found (as has been the case in England (UEA 2007)) that it was possible to change divisive cultures to more of a 'we' position if fair formulas were developed concerning shared budgets, if risk/reward was shared (e.g. in relation to under and overspend) and informal approaches (e.g. virtually aligned budgets/annual mapping) were flexibly utilised to support specific activities and coordinated provision.

However, in England attempts at more systematic approaches have encountered problems. For example, the national evaluation of Children's Trusts found that there were problems setting up formal budget pools and that there needed to be clarity concerning purpose, contracts, management, performance measures and participation (UEA 2007). In Dunlean (Chapter 2) regular problems arose, e.g. when agreements to share resources were not fulfilled, because crises arose that took staffing, time and energy away to single-agency issues. Indeed, there was resistance (as was found to be the case elsewhere (Anning et al. 2006)) to the suggestions that different services could become one organisation or one pot of resources could be set aside in order to enhance service delivery. For example, managers in Dunlean varied in their commitment to recommendations that suggested resources should be specifically set aside in local authorities for early intervention services (Munroe 2011). In particular, disagreements arose concerning the need to fund greater levels of acute and child protection services versus the need to intervene earlier.

The concept of variety lies at the heart of systems theory and complexity theory. These approaches have argued that uncertainty, risk and conflict are a central aspect of organisations (Lawler and Bilson 2010; Munroe 2011). They have suggested that creativity should be encouraged at all levels of an organisation (Bilson and Ross 1999; Lawler and Bilson 2010) and that public service organisations should become more able to absorb variety into their systems (Seddon 2008).

This type of writing replaced notions of management control with the idea of flat hierarchies, reflexivity and creativity. In has been connected to a number of management techniques. For example, soft systems methodology includes a seven-step model that identifies, develops and draws on a rich picture of a problem and formulates models/ways to express and transform the problem. Central to the process is the idea that any problem must be analysed in terms of the different worldviews, constraints and responsibilities experienced by customers, workers, departments, organisations and environments. Groups discuss, debate and compare the models that have been developed around a problem and then adapt the models to ensure they are culturally sensitive and systemically feasible before taking action to improve the situation (Checkland and Scholes 1990; Lawler and Bilson 2010).

Critical systems theory developed from a critique of soft systems approaches which suggested that they were unable to deal with issues of power (Jackson 1991; Lawler and Bilson 2010). Drawing on the work of Habermas (1984) critical systems theory concentrated on the need to see both strengths and weaknesses in organisations (Lawler and Bilson 2010). It took the position that different methodologies had different strengths and could be used in complementary rather than competing ways (Lawler and Bilson 2010). It was argued that no one paradigm should be allowed to override others and that the aim of organisations should be to achieve the maximisation of the potential of their workers (Lawler and Bilson 2010). Critical system theory approaches utilised contrasting organisational metaphors (e.g. machine/organism) to help people think creatively about political and human aspects of their organisation (Morgan 1986; Lawler and Bilson 2010).

Models such as the Vanguard 'check' model emerged that looked at the purpose of an organisation in relation to the frequency of service user demand, analysed the capacity of the system to respond, channelled product/expertise flow, identified waste, understood the system conditions that inhibit the flow of resources to the necessary places and promoted cooperative management thinking (Seddon 2008). Seddon (2008 drawing on Deming 1982) contrasted systems theory with hierarchical approaches. He suggested that the role of managers in the former was to manage work as functional activities but in the latter was to establish processes that helped us to collectively better understand performance and manage the flow of work through the system.

Seddon's (2008) approach was heavily influenced by Taiichi Ohno who developed the Toyota Production System (TPS) and believed that cost was associated with the way a variety of products (not mass-produced) flowed to the customer. In particular, this approach introduced the idea that products should only be made just in time (in response to customer demand), production should work within tolerances (rather than with blueprints or standards) and customer demand should pull materials through the system (Seddon 2008). In service industries this required staff and managers to reconceptualise problems and think of 'flow' as pulling expertise through the system to the service user to resolve issues more efficiently and at an earlier stage without being moved to the back office (Seddon 2008). The organisation needed to be able to respond to what mattered to the service user in order for them to get an appropriate service (e.g. if demand changed, the system changed (Seddon 2008)). Resources were not wasted because the service user got what mattered to them first time or as early as possible (this was referred to as 'pull value') and therefore resources did not need to be wasted on giving them an inappropriate service which was referred to as failure demand (Seddon 2008).

This approach required a system that was capable of providing a variety of responses, developed service user typologies to understand demand, had managers who were aware of failure demand (particularly in the public sector), involved cooperation, had an ethos of learning, was adaptive and involved intrinsic motivation (workers enjoy what they do) rather than extrinsic motivation (workers are stimulated by rewards or punishments) (Seddon 2008). This approach challenged the technical rational approach that suggested workers were lazy and rejected the notion that improvement requires an organisation to have new blood. In contrast it argued that the system inhibits people's contribution, managers should act on the system (all things out of the control of the worker) not the people, that staff should be trained in response to demand (in relation to the issues that come from service users), the worker should be the inspector (should be responsible for his/her own development and must get help for issues that they cannot solve), the focus should shift to prevention from inspection, there should be a movement from performance measures/ targets to measuring the real time a task takes and there should be greater understanding of worker/organisational capacity (the amount of things a person can do) (Seddon 2008). At the heart of this approach was the notion that there should be good jobs (jobs that people actually enjoy doing because they were proud of responding in a way that matters to the service user).

The forums in Pentesk provided an opportunity for groups of professionals and service providers to start to work in more systemic ways and to develop better understandings of what services worked. This led to a reduction in waste. However, it should be noted that this did not mean that great amounts of resources were suddenly freed up to go elsewhere in the local authority. Complexity theories (including chaos theory) have considered the social world as a complex adaptive system. They have been concerned with the idea that the system is self-organised, is a holistic/emergent entity, involves connections, is influenced by interdependence, is open (not involving equilibrium), is adaptable, is evolving, is dependent on history and involves many possible paths (Waldrop 1992; Mitleton-Kelly 2003; Lawler and Bilson 2010). This was very apparent at Pentesk when the social context of the provision changed. Multi-professional services are open to the vagaries of society and the recession caused by the banking system struck just as the forums were starting to act in the ways that had first been intended. Unemployment, repossessions and family pressures led to an increase in cases and increased pressure on the system hence initial resource gains were quickly used up and questions arose over whether the devolved management structures would have to be cut.

 Activity

Consider what motivates you to do your job. Compare your own ideas to those of your colleagues. What issues arise? Can you visit an integrated team and observe their work, processes and different spaces for dialogue? Can you discuss with team members the issues that motivate them and their work? What are the different intrinsic and extrinsic issues that arise? Can you consider how your ideas and the ideas of your colleagues relate to the aspirations of service users?

Multi-professional systems, relationships and change

The turbulent climate that surrounds multi-professional working raises an important issue of whether organisations ever reach a static state, achieve consensus and work without internal contradictions. In the case of Pentesk, the initiative developed differently at different levels within the overall organisation. Change (based on reflexive approaches) was stimulated by:

- the adoption of strengths-based, social justice and anti-discriminatory approaches not just for service users but also for staff, consistency between aims and practice involving new forms of strengths-based assessment, and all staff, service users and community members becoming recognised as potential change agents

- multi-professional joint training, learning and development and team meetings where staff were encouraged to recognise and discuss their different skills, knowledge and values in order to develop a sense of the group through joint problem-solving, conflict resolution and risk assessment/planning

- having clear lines of management/accountability/support, examining, considering and regularly reviewing the fairness of processes that allocated workloads, and ensuring all staff felt accepted into teams, had regular appraisal/review, were offered appropriate opportunities for professional development and were offered the opportunity to take further qualifications. For example, non-degree practitioners were provided with a career structure, including the opportunity to achieve/improve their professional status by obtaining a part-time BA Childhood Practice degree with a Scottish university.

Managers drew from a range of sources when planning these processes. Their approach can be connected to writing that has suggested we can foster multi-professional working by breaking down professional barriers and standardised approaches in the public sector (Bertram et al. 2002; Gilbert and Bainbridge 2003; Leathard 2003b; Tomlinson 2003; Harker et al. 2004; Frost 2005; Milne 2005; Anning et al. 2006; Scott 2006; Fitzgerald and Kay 2008; Glenny and Roaf 2008; Stone and Rixon 2008; Walker 2008; Lawler and Bilson 2010).

The new initiative in Pentesk adopted a systematic approach to building relationships and to discussing issues of conflict, workload allocations and various responses based on the abilities of diverse team and extended team members. Textbook/dogmatic approaches were jettisoned, theories that underpinned practice from different professional initial training were examined and analysed to establish their pros and cons, and the concept of expert knowledge was widened to include the views of the community, families, children and young people.

The strength of systemic approaches is believed to lie in their ability to enable complex problem-solving involving trusting, valuing and egalitarian relationships. However, for these approaches to be effective they require that the models developed for discussion do not become too prescriptive, normative or ideal and that they do not simply reproduce existing rules (Lawler and Bilson 2010).

A major critique of critical systems theory is that it values diversity so much that it accepts the persistence of approaches that are contradictory to its own ideals (e.g. hard systems approaches that iron out diversity), fail to challenge ingrained ideas of uniformity in organisations and therefore fail to fulfil its aim of worker 'emancipation' and often reproduce the very conditions it is trying to avoid (Mingers 1992; Tsoukas 1993; Taket and White 2000; Lawler and Bilson 2010). Indeed, grand and totalising theories often have such problems (Davis and Watson 2002).

It is argued that critical systems theory does not do enough to move beyond uniform approaches, highlight the interconnectedness of people in organisations/systems, critique linear approaches to organisational management and ask us to recognise the connections between people and environments. In particular, this critique promotes the alternative idea that we should do away with all conformity and organisations could be made up of networks of conversations that involve a dispersal of responsibility, reduce the restrictions set on workers, promote inspiring relationships and enable change to come from local critical reflection (Bateson 1973; Maturana and Bunnell 1998; Lawler and Bilson 2010).

Critiques of systems theory can be connected with postmodern notions from which a conception of ethical management has evolved that attempts to balance the influence of external frameworks with the local values, views and practices of individual workers and their managers (e.g. concerning inclusiveness, liberation, emancipation, etc.). Like systems theory postmodern ideas point out the need to move to more plural, relativist, complex and reflexive frameworks that recognise the spontaneous nature of our work, persuade us to reflect on emotions/actions (our own and other people's) and encourage us to respect other viewpoints (though not to accept everything other people do) (Bauman 1993; Lawler and Bilson 2010).

Like systems theory, they promote the analysis of the subjective nature of managers, teams, values, cultures and histories at the same time as encouraging us to consider the possibility of different forms of action that question power relations and enable us to take responsibility for our own work (Lawler and Bilson 2010). Postmodern approaches share the systems theory idea that we should enable workers to take more responsibility and encourage organisations to stimulate more enjoyable working (Seddon 2008). At the centre of this way of thinking is the idea that we should resist management fads, recognise that change is a continuous process not a time-limited project, be aware that workers may be at the stage of initiative fatigue, and realise that textbook ideas and ideal types don't transfer well (Buchanan et al. 1999; Adams 1996; Shapiro 1996).

However, unlike systems theory, postmodern approaches are much more focused on rejecting consensus and promoting political dialogue, analysis and 'give and take' concerning different people's ideas, aspirations and requirements. For example, Davis (2011) utilises a range of authors to discuss postmodern approaches to integrated children's services. He explains a shift in thinking by professionals that enables them to consider issues of power/politics (pose questions concerning who defines the identity of service users) at the same time as following systems theory ideas that challenges ideas of hierarchy (e.g. critique systems that privileges the role of the professional), promote participation (the possibility of collaborative practice) and questions authority/truth (recognises the expertise of all service users).

This work encourages you to avoid seeing service users, workers and managers as victims of systems (Corker and Shakespeare 2001; Davis 2011). It suggests that the antidote to greater surveillance and assessment of professionals could come in the form of collective action, knowledge legitimisation and political struggle (Lawler and Bilson 2010; Penna and O'Brien 1996). This work destabilises notions of uniformity/consensus and recognises the necessity for us to create the potential for unconventional political outcomes in multi-professional processes (Penna and O'Brien 1996).

This writing encourages us to rethink the way we look at service provisions. The use of such approaches in Pentesk drew on the idea that different social actors react in different ways in any specific situation and, therefore, any approach to multi-disciplinary working will not necessarily work in the same way, in the same context, on separate occasions (Davis 2007, 2011). The development of complex integrated professional roles was found to have had a positive impact on families in Pentesk (Smith and Davis 2010). It was found that in spite of some local service intransigence, the multi-agency forums were extremely highly evaluated (by participants) and enabled the new service to engage with a range of people (including children and parents) in discussions about assessment, planning and delivery (Smith 2009; Smith and Davis 2010). Despite occasional difficulties (with regard to a lack of resources, agencies not undertaking agreed work, etc.), the forums enabled 'joined-up' planning and support for children and young people. The initiative resulted in improved communication, enabled the development of shared understandings and removed the likelihood that a single agency would be left to support complex cases on its own (Smith 2009; Smith and Davis 2010).

The local forums and teams were able to act as a collective catalyst for change. Smith and Davis (2010) concluded that a combination of practice (streamlined and complex assessments), culture (shared vision established by training) and systems change (devolved management and dialogue) had enabled the multi-professional initiative in Pentesk to organically grow. This growth came about when participants recognised that that not all staff and managers in a system have the same conceptual, practical or intellectual starting points or that any one individual has totalising power. This suggests (in keeping with Davis 2007, 2011) that it is possible to develop a social dynamic approach to children's services that rejects the notion that any person in the system is permanently powerless and breaks down stereotypes (e.g. concerning different professionals and children) by recognising the complex and diverse abilities of staff, parents, professionals, children, young people and communities and fostering innovative, creative and unusual responses to people's life problems that take account of those abilities.

Professionals in Pentesk should not now be faced with the problems that emerged in Dunlean because they can sit down at an early stage with families, identify their life issues (e.g. that there is conflict in the family), use assessment procedures to explain how different family members are feeling (identify emotional fear, hopes, aspirations) and identify local solutions (protective factors such as friends, relatives, local groups) and develop relatively quick and appropriate collaborative plans for support (counselling, housing, transport, health services, etc.). In each specific family the actual plan will be different and take account of diverse cultural issues and contexts, and each plan will be reviewed regularly and reformed.

The concept of diversity (pluralism) (Lawler and Bilson 2010) needs a little unpacking here. Young (1990) argued that the collective deliberation of problems in institutions should not require people to always come to collective consensus because she felt that this denied difference. Yet the suggestion that organisations should value difference and reject all truths has been criticised as leading to inertia because there is so much diversity no one knows where to start their work from (Lawler and Bilson 2010; Davis 2011). Recognising this criticism we (drawing on Bauman 1993; Lawler and Bilson 2010) encourages you to think of consensus and diversity, not as opposites, but simply as frameworks of thought that influence the way we plan our work and analyse things that we encounter on a daily basis. For example, in previous chapters we suggested that multi-professional plans should take account of workers' capacities and organisational contexts. Postmodern approaches help us recognise that this is a political process and that the information can be used against workers or agencies in processes of stigmatisation where their capacity is compared to the capacity of other people or organisations. We hope that the ideas in this book help you avoid such practices and recognise that capacity issues can be positively discussed as part of constant cycles of learning/renewal (Percy-Smith et al. 2001, Kirby et al. 2003).

 Activity

Can you think of different approaches that might help develop your organisation and the individuals within? Do service plans take account of worker, service user and agency capacity and diversity? Are service users offered a variety of provisions or do standardised approaches dominate? Are there spaces for problem-solving/modelling processes? Do you carry out trust-building exercises? Are people viewed as having collective responsibility for change?

Conclusion

This chapter has encouraged you to recognise that leadership in your workplace can be provided by a range of people irrespective of personal cultures, professional backgrounds or managerial positions. It concludes that change processes can be collaborative and should recognise the diverse perspectives of those involved in multi-disciplinary services. We described how the collective, reflexive and interrelational approaches to service assessment and planning at Pentesk enabled coordinated multi-professional working to emerge in the integrated teams and forums (e.g. through joint training, trust-building processes, knowledge sharing, joint problem-solving, etc.).

The chapter critiqued notions of top-down management and promoted the adoption of approaches that embrace diversity, complexity and change. It demonstrated that practice, culture and systems change had organically grown in Pentesk that enabled staff to overcome initial barriers such as professional hierarchies, agency demarcation and worker capacity. It also suggested that the forums in Pentesk had enabled participants to better understand the complex and diverse abilities of staff, parents, professionals, children, young people and communities. The chapter compared and contrasted systemic and postmodern approaches to demonstrate the need to balance ideas of consensus and diversity and concluded that postmodern techniques have value in multi-professional settings (e.g. that involve several organisations with different capacities) when they are utilised as a tool for understanding and not as a prescriptive approach.

 ## Recommended further reading

Lawler, J. and Bilson, A. (2010) *Social Work Management and Leadership: Managing Complexity with Creativity.* Abingdon: Routledge.

Mullins, L. J. (2005) *Management and Organisational Behaviour.* London: Prentice Hall.

Seddon, J. (2008) *Systems Thinking in the Public Sector: The Failure of the Reform Regime . . . and a Manifesto for a Better Way.* Axminster: Triarchy Press.

6

Multi-professional evaluation

Chapter Overview

This chapter critiques concepts of total quality management and research-based evaluation by suggesting that such approaches are problematic because they are not sufficiently participatory, impose objective measures and put too much reliance on outsiders who do not have an understanding of local context. This chapter utilises a case study from a Welsh inclusion project in a local authority (we have called Penwall) that, for example enabled children and young people to define their own measures of success, in order to encourage you to move towards more relational approaches to evaluation. It concludes that if we aim to develop more inclusive multi-disciplinary services then we should also ensure those services enable collaborative dialogue concerning the measures that we use for evaluation, build sustained structures of participation and foster strong relationships of evaluation. (Note that the aim of this chapter is to consider the pros and cons of different types of evaluation of practice and not to give an extensive tutorial on research methods, roles, tools, ethics, etc. which we have covered elsewhere, e.g. Tisdall et al. (2009)).

Case Study

The Penwall case study analyses an evaluation of a Welsh multi-agency inclusion project. The project aimed to find out the views of children in order to further develop policies and services on inclusion and to consider how longer-term evaluation processes could be put in place that were underpinned by notions of collaboration and participation. In this chapter we will consider the extent to which service providers were enabled to develop a collaborative process of evaluation with disabled children and young people.

Total quality management

It has been suggested there is a continuum of research-related approaches stretching from hard (quantitative) evidence-led performance management to soft evidence-based approaches that involve interpretive designs, dialogue and discussion (Frost 2005). Soft evidence approaches also included the notion that the practitioner should draw upon research literature to decide how to plan services.

It was argued that both approaches had problems. Hard evidence approaches encountered problems because their use of objective methods (e.g. randomised control trials) did not fit well with complex contexts and soft evidence-based research encountered difficulties with the huge volume of research to be considered on a topic (Frost 2005). Both approaches tended to lead to the codification of knowledge where ideas/knowledge were written down as apparently neutral facts, used to create typical responses to apparently neutral questions/problems and taught to professionals/students as unproblematic. These methods were criticised for failing to enable local questioning of implicit and explicit assumptions (Frost 2005).

Similarly, this raised issues concerning the concept of quality. Definitions included reliability (how consistently a thing is achieved), appropriateness (the extent to which a need is satisfied) and value (economic, social or political worth) (Bank 1992; McIver 2002; Dahlberg et al. 2007). Writers differentiated between ideas of quality that were concerned with conformance to standards, specification or purpose (technical approaches), reduction of cost/expense (value approaches) and those that adopted more interrelational approaches that attempted to engage with service users' perspectives (user approaches) (McIver 2002).

It became apparent that statistical performance indicators were just one type of evaluation that shouldn't be privileged over others. Writers contrasted summative (measurements) and formative (developmental) forms of evaluation and argued, for example, that there were many different things that could be evaluated including cost/efficiency (resources in relation to gain/loss), outcome (whether anything changed), impact (the specific effect the initiative had), implementation (whether the initiative actually delivered to the intended audience or in the intended way), logic (the theory a process was based on), need (actual problems) or design (the planning/development/delivery process) (Rossi et al. 2004; Jones and Leverett 2008).

Over time it became possible to differentiate between voluntary and imposed evaluations of quality (McIver 2002). For example, the total quality management model was established as a voluntary ongoing continuous learning process that focused on customer satisfaction and delight (Morgan and Murgatroyd 1994; Wilding 1994). There were two main strands of this type of quality management: the International Organisation for Standardisation (ISO) and the European Foundation for Quality Management (EFQM – also known as the Business Excellence Model) (McIver 2002).

The ISO 9000 encouraged companies to set up step-by step processes to identify the goals they wanted to achieve (e.g. efficiency, better services, customer satisfaction, increased market share, improved communication, etc.), what others expected of the organisation (e.g. customers, suppliers, service users, society, shareholders, employees, etc.) and who would analyse the organisations' current status (e.g. self-assessment, external assessment, customer assessment) (ISO 2004). The ISO process aimed to enhance effectiveness and efficiency in relation to well-defined organisational objectives including better integration/alignment of planning for achievement, consistent organisational performance, more transparent and participatory operations, more effective use of resources, more prioritised initiatives and greater predictability of results (ISO 2004). Setting aside the tautological (repetitious) nature of these aims it is very difficult at first glance to see the ISO agenda as problematic; however, they tended to encounter a range of practical issues (including staff reacting to them being utilised in a top-down manner) (Seddon 2008). In contrast to ISO, the EFQM model sought to integrate notions of leadership, change, innovation planning, governance and efficiency with contemporary ideas concerning sustainability, inclusion, diversity, creativity, flexibility, agility and stakeholder involvement (McIver 2002).

Such approaches to quality management highlighted the need to include service users in processes that defined the way that quality should be measured (Dahlberg et al. 2007). An effort was made to separate out technical and value definitions of quality that had more relevance for infrastructure projects and those approaches that were more useful for face-to-face services (McIver 2002). Face-to-face approaches to quality also drew from humanistic/systems ideas of management (discussed in Chapter 4) to promote quality within the context of contemporary ideas of collaborative leadership, teamwork and continuous improvement (McIver 2002).

We can see such ideas in Penwall where Welsh devolution had led to the development of a number of new policy initiatives. In particular and in an attempt to put 'rights into action' the Welsh legislators had developed the 'Core Aims for Children and Young People in Wales' document that suggested that children should get a flying start to life including:

- a comprehensive range of education, training and learning opportunities

- the best possible health free from abuse, victimisation and ex-ploitation

- play, leisure, sporting and cultural activities

- treated with respect and have their race and cultural identity recognised

- a safe home and community

- not to be disadvantaged by poverty.

(WAG 2004)

These initiatives were to be judged by a combination of hard SMART (specific, measurable, accurate, realistic and timed) indicators and softer qualitative indicators. Quantitative indicators/outcomes included recording the number of deaths, illness, exam results, accidents, etc. and qualitative indicators included children's views on participation, access to services, feelings of self-confidence and fulfilment of life issues (WAG 2004).

Similarly, Penwall's inclusion policy stated a commitment to quality educational opportunities for all its children and young people, enshrined the notion that children with additional support requirements should be educated with their peer group and stipulated that the first point of specialist provision should occur in local mainstream schools. These initiatives undertook to ensure that disabled children and children receiving additional support experienced equality in schools/public authorities, that services promoted positive attitudes to disabled people and that disabled people were to be safe, e.g. from harassment/bullying (WAG 2008). In relation to schooling it was argued that definitions of learning requirements were to be holistic; practitioners were asked to consider the thinking behind practice and not simply to concentrate on deficit perspectives (WAG 2008). Such approaches connected to discussions in Chapter 2 (assessment) and Chapter 3 (participation) which sought to encourage multi-professional working to adopt politically nuanced, holistic and strengths-based approaches.

However, it should also be recognised that the top-down nature of national policies on inclusion can mean that there are tensions between processes that aim to standardise the quality of provision and approaches that seek to promote local participatory service development. Chapter 4 (traditional management) critiqued standardised and hierarchical approaches to service development, including the sorts of technical rational ideas that underpinned ISO while Chapter 5 (contemporary management) called for collaborative approaches to service delivery that recognised the ability of children, families, communities and professionals. These chapters were particularly critical of the idea that leadership in multi-professional settings should be left in the hands of individual managers. The EFQM model aimed to avoid such problems by creating excellence through enabling organisations to role-model vision, inspiration, integrity and better managed processes. The EFQM model highlighted the need to nurture relationships and there was a much greater degree of self-assessment in EFQM than the ISO approach (McIver 2002). Self-assessment involved a RADAR (results, approach, deployment, assessment and review) technique for defining what results organisations wanted to achieve, planning/designing/developing approaches that would deliver results and deploying/assessing/refining these techniques to enable sustainability.

Total quality management referred to the set of RADAR-inspired behaviours, activities and initiatives that sought to achieve excellence and delight stakeholders (EFQM 2011). Great emphasis was placed on the role of leaders to set the culture, vision and goals (EFQM 2011). However, this also meant there remained a tendency for the approach to include an element of top-down prescription (Seddon 2008). The consequence in the public sector of such approaches as the EFQM business excellence model was that below national level local authorities were required (in the name of continuous improvement) to carry out performance reviews, respond to national performance indicators, establish local performance processes, develop service plans and publish annual performance results (McIver 2002). These approaches have been heavily criticised (in a manner similar to top-down management discussed in Chapter 4) for leading to too much concentration on process and not enough development of staff knowledge and skills (Munroe 2011).

 Activity

What is your approach to evaluation? Have you experience of using performance indicators? How relevant are indicators such as rates of teen pregnancy, levels of child abuse, numbers of school drop-outs, birth weights, intensities of drug use to your work? Can you identify guidance in local and national policy documents for how people in your profession should carry out evaluations? Do you have specific approaches in your workplace/places you have been on placement? Could you look up a research methods book to discover what they say about the difference between soft/qualitative and hard/quantitative indicators (e.g. Bell 1999; Agar 1996)? Could you discuss with your work colleagues and service users what the key indicators of success should be in your workplaces? If you are a student could you consider how teaching staff ask you to evaluate their courses, for example do you fill in a sheet at the end of term or the national student survey? How useful is this exercise?

Research-based evaluation/development

At the same time as the concept of quality appeared an alternative discourse emerged which highlighted ideas of research, evidenced-base working and collaborative development. Many authors highlighted the importance of research as a means of monitoring and evaluating practice (OECD 2001b; Gasper 2010). It was suggested that evaluation could be carried out by a range of people (e.g. practitioners, independent researchers, other professionals, consultants, inspectors, peers) and could occur at different levels (e.g. governmental, local authority, agency/service, practitioner and service user (Jones and Leverett 2008). This gave a focus for multi-professional initiatives that employed evaluators and independent researchers to carry out a range of duties including evaluating whether an initiative worked, employment in an advisory role (e.g. to support service development) or working on recommending new ways to do things (Jones and Leverett 2008).

Some authors criticised outsider evaluation arguing that multi-professional practice that took a hands-on approach to evaluation was more likely to be able to use the evaluation to improve practice and that many external researchers lacked reflexive capacities (Bruner 1996; Finer and Hundt 2000). Practitioner research (connected to processes of mentoring) that analysed theory and practice was highlighted as an important aspect of service development and as affording sound possibilities for learning (Gasper 2010). Rather than relying on outsiders, shying away from evaluation or feeling it was a daunting prospect you were encouraged to take more of a hands-on role in the evaluation process (Bruner 1996). Specifically, multi-professional working was encouraged to utilise research and evaluation to dismantle traditional forms of organisation/practice and reassemble them into new possibilities (Gasper 2010). Research/evaluation was perceived to offer strong support to the development of multi-professional services because it held the potential to enable participants to unpack different people's understandings concerning team work, assessment, specialism, etc. (Glenny and Roaf 2008).

It was argued that various actors' experience/knowledge could form the basis for service evaluation if the organisation did not solely rely on rational objective research (Lawler and Bilson 2010). Such writers promoted individual and group reflexive approaches (discussed in the previous chapter) as a way of stimulating evidence-informed practice (Lawler and Bilson 2010). Catchy acronyms were developed including RIPE which encouraged us to make decisions that recognised the complex interplay between **R**esearch/evaluation, **I**deological positions, **P**olitical disputes and **E**conomic realities (Frost 2005). This approach challenged attempts by proponents of evidence-led practice and performance indicator notions of quality to impose uni-causal, static and rationalist ideas on public services (Frost 2005; Seddon 2008). Such approaches encouraged practitioners to examine disputes concerning the distribution of power and decision-making in public services and raised questions concerning how you should consider issues of evaluation and how able you were to question your own practices.

In the case of the Penwall evaluation the local authority managers combined internal evaluation processes with an outsider evaluator project that hoped to develop a more in-depth understanding of children's views of the services they experienced. External evaluation involved researchers carrying out questionnaires with children and young people. The questionnaire was developed in consultation with service providers, piloted with young people and followed up with focus groups. Despite the piloting process, the questionnaire was mainly an adult construction.

In Chapter 2 (assessment) and Chapter 3 (participation) we contrasted medicalised notions of impairment with social model, ecological and strengths-based approaches. The questionnaire tended to centre around medicalised notions of impairment (e.g. asking questions about whether the children had learning requirements, questions concerning what their impairment diagnosis was and questions on the effect of the impairment on handwriting, use of equipment and on physical activities in specific subjects).

The questionnaire seemed to make the assumption that the pupils required specialised support (e.g. posing questions about whether they needed help at school or needed to be withdrawn from mainstream classes, whether they got help during tests, whether teachers understood their difficulties and whether they had fallen behind in their school work). Such approaches to research have been heavily criticised in disability research for focusing on the disabled person's limitations and assuming they are a social victim at the expense of enquiring whether disabled people actually experience barriers related to the contemporary organisation of society (Abberley 1987, 1992; Oliver 1990; Finkelstein 1993; Campbell and Oliver 1996; Barnes et al. 1999).

Some more social model type questions were asked concerning whether specialist staff created barriers that prevented them from interacting with other pupils and whether teaching staff listened to their views but no questions were asked about the children's strengths and capability to contribute in a meaningful way to the development of their peer group, schools, families, communities and services. The evaluative process (despite the piloting phase) also failed to develop questions from the service users' perspectives.

From a quantitative perspective it was possible to answer the questions in a bland 'tick box' yes/no manner and some of the questions would have benefited from using a numbered ranking/scales approach (e.g. 1–5, 1–10) (Bell 1999) or a folk estimate(e.g. the 'how often/many' type approach) (Agar 1996) that would have given more depth to the children's responses and enabled the consultant to gauge their level of feeling on different topics (e.g. to show how effective they perceived teaching, community, out-of-school, social work and therapy services to be). From a qualitative perspective the evaluation could have used alternative methods such as a grid life history approach that would have focused on understanding key moments in the children and young people's lives (Bell 1999) or used longer-term methods of informal participatory interviewing that would have enabled participants to share life experiences (over days and weeks), to develop rapport with respondents by exchanging experiences and to allow respondents to set the agenda, explore complex meanings and unpack the logic of situations (Agar 1996).

The questionnaire involved little understanding of the conceptual issues involved in disability research that, for example, contrast medical model perspectives that focus on impairment with social model ideas that define disability as the social barriers that people create which limit the lives of disabled people (Abberley 1987; Oliver 1990; Finkelstein 1993; Campbell and Oliver 1996; Barnes et al. 1999). As such the external evaluation was limited in its ability to contribute to sustained change and to developments that would help to fulfil Penwall's expectation that inclusive services should be based on the social model of disability. This contrast is demonstrated in Table 6.1 by means of a set of indicators developed by Davis (2001) with children to analyse the experience of disabled children in mainstream play provisions. A similar set of contrasting indicators could have been used to investigate children's experience of multi-professional services (see Table 6.2).

Table 6.1 Comparison of deficit and positive indicators of play

Medical/deficit model *Negative indicators*	Social model *Positive indicators*
Play space is only about education or therapy.	Play is for fun.
Adults dominate the space.	Children have choices.
Adults play for 'special needs' children.	Adults interact with all children.
'Special needs' children only play with adults.	Disabled children choose who they play with.
'Special needs' children play in specific rooms.	Disabled children have access to all the rooms.
'Special needs' children only play with 'their' equipment.	All children share equipment.
'Special needs' children are restricted by rules.	Sensitive guidelines apply to all children.
Non-'special needs' children take on 'carer' roles with disabled children.	Children have a variety of relationships.
Therapists set the play programme.	Children choose what they want to do.
Adults control the short- and long-term agenda.	Children's ideas influence decision-making/children help run the club.
The play programme activities take no account of age/preference.	Children participate in age-appropriate/preference-related play.
The clubs are overcrowded and disabled children are restricted to specific areas.	Clubs have plenty of space and children can move about freely.
The 'special needs' children are treated as precious.	All children's differences are valued.

Table 6.2 Comparison of deficit and positive indicators of multi-professional evaluation

Medical/deficit model *Negative indicators*	**Social model** *Positive indicators*
Service providers do not consult children and assume that disabled children are not able to put forward opinions.	Service providers use a range of verbal, textual, creative and non-verbal participatory approaches.
Service providers only consult the child's parents, guardians or relatives.	Children have choices on how to participate, their views are compared with those of their parents, siblings, family members, members of their community and professionals.
Service providers tell the parents there is limited funding available and offer a limited number of choices.	There is dialogue concerning the social context within which children make their personal choices and services are designed around their aspirations and ways of being in the world.
Professionals assume they are the experts.	The expertise of different people is openly discussed, different options are fully explained and there is considered/informed choice.
Service providers assume disabled children live in a vacuum and do not communicate with their peer group.	Participatory peer group approaches are employed that enable well resourced, creative and artistic dialogue. Solutions to issues of inclusion are collaboratively modelled, tried out and adapted.
Professionals control the evaluation process.	The process of service development involves creative co-construction and all participants are enabled to take leadership roles at different times in the process.
Solutions are taken from an individualist list of medical model research literature that underplays the ability of disabled children, their parents, peer group and communities.	Unexpected solutions arise as a result of enjoyable, innovative, local and community based discussions. National and international examples of creative and collaborative solutions are discussed, analysed and adapted.

The key difference between these two approaches is the perception that disabled children are able to connect in an inclusive way with other people. Inclusion has been defined as requiring pluracy and equity of experience (Evans and Lunt 2002; Ainscow and Booth 2003). From that starting point social model type approaches enable no end of creative possibilities to emerge.

 Activity

What is your approach to evaluation? Have you experience of using performance indicators or developing practitioner research? (If you are a student are you planning a project that is to be assessed?) What types of questions will you use? Consider the two sides of Tables 6.1 and 6.2 for a moment. Another difference between the two columns concerns the time and effort involved. How able are you and your colleagues to develop such processes? Can you work with/receive support from other local organisations that understand the context of these children's lives (rather than external consultants)?

Relational approaches to evaluation

The Penwall external evaluation lacked a collaborative feel. Findings were put forward to suggest what needed changing (bullies, lack of staff training and more flexible curriculum) but by asking abstract, 'what's wrong with you, other pupils, teachers, etc.?' type questions concerning impairment and special requirements the project initially failed to investigate more fundamental questions concerning how approaches/services might change and who should change them.

The questionnaire missed an opportunity to talk to the children about the context of policy/practice development and to consider creative solutions and approaches that were collaborative/integrative. For example, there was a potential that the questionnaire collected criticism of professionals that was uncontextualised and that would stoke up disagreement, conflict and discord rather than dialogue. The process failed to create spaces where practitioners, parents, children, peer group and community groups actually collaborated on evaluating the services. Nor did it encourage practitioners to analyse their practice in an individually reflexive way or participants to be involved in group reflexive moments.

Systemic and social network theories have critiqued the use of performance indicators and deficit model approaches to the evaluation of staff in the public sector. They question whether it is possible in the public sector to develop fixed and universally applicable sets of criteria for evaluating services (Boyne 2002). Some writers argue that definitions of quality depend on the nature of the service and the values/expectations of stakeholders (McIver 2002). In a similar way the evaluator's report for Penwall failed to creatively engage with a range of stakeholders in Penwall.

The questionnaire was carried out over a short time period and was utilised by managers/officers to gauge the climate of inclusion. Managers were aware that more participatory and sustained approaches would have to be developed and had an aspiration (enshrined in local policies) to develop community-based approaches to participatory evaluation (similar to those utilised in Durham in Chapter 3).

The external evaluation mainly resorted to examining satisfaction issues. Satisfaction surveys in multi-professional services have been perceived to be problematic because the public sector is based on complex service relationships, partnerships, professionalism and the concept that the customer can be a potential co-producer of services (McIver 2002). In the Penwall case the potential was overlooked for children to be participatory co-producers of the evaluation report (as had been the case in Durham in Chapter 3) and the questionnaire only characterised disabled children as service users and professional adults as service providers. This meant the potential for creative co-delivery or development of services initially went overlooked.

This occurred because the external evaluation failed to follow the example of the Durham case study and spend time building participatory relationships of evaluation. That is, despite attempts to adopt social model approaches by staff in Penwall and develop more sustained approaches, the external researchers were not well placed to help develop embedded structures that would enable children and families to be consistently involved over the long term in service assessment, planning and delivery (O'Neil 2002; Ball 2003; Watson 2003; Bruner 2006; Dahlberg et al. 2007; Glenny and Roaf 2008; Davis 2011).

Evaluation is very much a complex process dependent on people's subjective perspectives (Wilding 1994). A focus on one set of measurements can create unintended perverse incentives (Freeman 2002; McIver 2002; Seddon 2008). The initial questionnaire tried to respond to the Welsh policy context that aimed to produce services and education processes that were more inclusive of disabled children but it failed to develop a participatory and joint learning process, to make obvious issues of uncertainty and to utilise them as tools for joint and co-constructed analysis. The external evaluation followed the problems of other studies that have failed to step out of the norm (Perri6 et al. 2002; Dahlberg et al. 2007). The fundamental problem with such external evaluations is that they fail to begin the process of project design from the perspective that evaluation/leadership is a collaborative venture.

Seddon (2008) was scathing of performance management for similar reasons. He replaced the catchy acronyms of performance management with his own acronym DUMB (distorting, undermining, minister-inspired and blocking improvement). He cautioned that we should not allow plausible acronyms to fool us into believing that they involved a reliable method. Seddon (2003) criticised ISO 9000 for leading to a situation where managers assured quality rather than that services delivered what service users required. He criticised EFQM on the basis that its top-down criteria were employed as a starting point for analysis rather than the what and why of the service. Seddon (2003) believed that EFQM wording put pressure on managers to lead with vision, establish standards, agree targets, etc. in a way that emphasised hierarchy at the expense of seeing the organisation as a system that involves collaborative processes (Seddon 2003). We can see this problem with external evaluators who are commissioned for their expertise and can therefore assume they have an expert/ hierarchical position to fulfil.

The external evaluator, researcher or manager who adopts top-down evaluation techniques becomes more of an inspector than a facilitator. It has been argued that such a role can create stress in organisations that are characterised by rules and hierarchy (Walshe and Shortell 2004; Jones and Leverett 2008). It has been argued that inspection approaches mostly have symbolic significance for service users and that it would be better for inspection processes to be based on self-assessment (in a similar way to the EFQM model) that stimulated dialogue between service user, providers and inspectors (Boyne et al. 2001; Brady 2004; Jones and Leverett 2008). Similarly, it has been suggested that inspection processes put too much emphasis on top-down management/regulation and that they often fail to listen to children, families and workers when they raise concerns regarding staff and organisational practice (Munroe 2011).

We encourage you (in a similar way to Chapter 3) to think about creating spaces for dialogue that recognise the complexity of public services and enable those involved to genuinely discuss difficult issues (Lawler and Bilson 2010). In particular, it has been argued that multi-professional processes and practice in children and family services need to be based more on feedback from service users and enable greater engagement with the rights, feelings and experiences of children and families (Munroe 2011). This raises the question about whether you feel able in your job to act on emotions, intuition and feelings. It also brings into question the nature of your organisation, for example whether the culture of your organisation enables reflexive understanding of workers' problems or is more concerned with apportioning blame (Lawler and Bilson 2010). In the last chapter we demonstrated the potential for multi-professional services to utilise local forums, teams and processes to enable appreciative practice (Glenny and Roaf 2008; Lawler and Bilson 2010). We suggested that multi-professional settings should utilise the leadership capacity of all the participants.

In Chapter 3 we saw how the approach in Durham had been built up over a period of time and that the One Stop process benefited from the experience that Investing in Children had of working across different services in the local authority. It is important to note that Penwall had a different starting point from Durham and that major policy shifts on additional support and integrated working had only recently occurred. Indeed, the local authority was in the process of developing more integrated structures and relationships. At the centre of this development was the creation of structures/processes that would encourage dialogue across different services and between service providers, children and families. This development was similar to changes that took place in Pentesk (Chapters 4 and 5). For example, there were a number of different approaches that aimed to develop more collaborative and multi-professional working. These included:

- local strategic partnerships and community strategies that ensured appropriate governance of organisations, produced a clear vision of what services were seeking to achieve and enabled the development of documentation on service delivery, planning and evaluation

- an accountability committee that scrutinised directorates and a local authority cabinet committee that reviewed policy, strategy and delivery proposals

- planning, review and evaluation partnerships that involved yearly meetings of school heads and inclusion service managers that examined issues of support for learners

- an additional support advisory group that required senior managers/ officers to be committed to working in partnership and to develop progressive leadership

- service level agreements between schools and the local authority, e.g. regarding inclusion support, guiding principals, arrangements for outreach and pupil placements in learning centres, etc.

- multi-agency agreements that identified shared values, understood pupil requirements, provided support/empowerment to service providers, promoted inclusion, improved prevention/early intervention, matched services/resources to requests, agreed performance measures, established evaluation mechanisms, outlined complaints/ dispute resolution procedures, enabled participation and ensured positive outcomes

- clear assessment systems, procedures and processes (including learner-centred planning) that collaboratively matched provision to individual requirements, defined the nature of meetings, explained the range of strategies/options available, appointed support coordinators/key workers, agreed the allocation of provision/ funding, outlined who was to be involved in delivery of services, stated when services were to be delivered, defined indicators/ outcomes of success, established exit criteria, and enabled learners to be central to processes of planning, target setting, decision-making, implementation and review

- locality/cluster groups involving expert professionals on inclusion who were tasked with promoting a culture of inclusion, increasing the recognition of diversity, fostering learner-centred working and providing outreach/early intervention (activities included cluster conferences, a staff support/training/development network, parent drop-in surgeries, parenting skills workshops, transition planning and a cluster-based referral system)

- locality multi-agency forums with community hubs that involved multi-professional teams (including education professionals, police, voluntary organisations, housing, family support, safeguarding, adult learning, youth work, educational welfare, social services and health services) that planned, commissioned and monitored integrated services

- integrated working frameworks and systems for coordination, information sharing and transition planning

- community-focused schools that promoted parent partnerships, community safety partnerships, improved sports facilities, adult learning initiatives, community regeneration and links with voluntary organisations, health boards, community learning services and services for elderly people

- a children and young people's partnership that was tasked with the role of identifying the needs of children, young people and families and developing plans/priorities for service providers using a four-tier model of frontline, additional, complex and acute provision and evaluated against criteria such as learning, safety, achievement, health, respect, confidence and self-reliance.

It was hoped that the shift to more integrated, multi-professional and relational forms of service delivery would enable practice to be streamlined, pupils to experience more age-appropriate/flexible provision and information to be accessed more quickly.

The local authority had a strong history of supporting disabled children and a great deal of professional expertise related to supporting children who experienced behavioural problems, autistic spectrum disorder, coordination difficulties, sensory 'difficulties', specific learning 'difficulties' and moderate learning 'difficulties'. Similarly, they had utilised a range of assessment tools (e.g. function/standardised tests of cognition, literacy, numeracy, emotional well-being, etc.) to identify/track children requiring additional support. However, there was uncertainty regarding how to marry this experience to the contemporary requirement to enable service users to develop their own ways to measure service quality. A key and continuing aspect of the changes in Penwall involved establishing how effectively children and young people were able to participate in processes that matched provision to their requirements. Such processes required professionals to question ideas concerning how they measure services.

For example, total quality management has been found to be problematic in public services because of difficulties encountered when trying to identify the consumer and agree what to measure

(Pollitt 1988; Dahlberg et al. 2007). It was found that in multi-professional settings the customer included a variety of people such as parents, carers, local community members and local agency staff (McIver 2002). A range of interested parties (e.g. consumers, taxpayers, staff and politicians) had to be involved in developing indicators for measurement and these different people employed a variety of contrasting criteria (e.g. quantity, speed of delivery, effectiveness) to judge performance (Boyne 2002). Different people's quality criteria included issues of accessibility, effectiveness, acceptability, equity, responsiveness, reliability and openness (McIver 2002).

Critiques of quality measurement have suggested that service providers have, in the past, not known what to measure (e.g. they have created targets irrespective of organisational capability to meet new aims or service user need) that managers have mistakenly assumed that targets motivated people, that services have focused too much on accountability related to bureaucratic processes (e.g. budget issues) and that work processes have become more and more prescriptive (e.g. managers assumed that targets were essential and forced this perspective onto workers) (Seddon 2008).

In Penwall a great deal of effort had been put into developing frameworks for quality management. This process included the development of well-being indicators related to a range of social (relationships, family, peers), physical (health, nutrition, exercise), emotional (confidence, esteem, resilience), cultural (identity, recognition and diversity) and learning (academic/practical skills and attributes) outcomes.

We can see connections here to forms of assessment in Chapter 2 that utilised the 'well-being triangle' and resilience matrix (Jack 1997; Daniel and Wassell 2002; Stradling et al. 2009). Such tools have tried to encourage professionals to approach assessment from the point of view of children's own aspirations to experience self-emancipation (be healthy, resilient, confident, independent, etc.), supportive relationships (that include guidance, understanding, safety, encouragement, etc.), structural/economic well-being (e.g. resources, housing, schooling, family, employment, etc.) and buffers to adversity (e.g. peer group support, strong local relationships, membership of clubs, etc.) (Jack 1997; Daniel and Wassell 2002; Stradling et al. 2009).

This suggests that there needs to be greater connection between policies, processes and practices related to additional support and those that promote multi-agency children's services. It is also important for you to recognise that processes of holistic/strengths-based assessment also require processes of holistic/strengths-based evaluation. Various professionals in Penwall were trying to sensitively balance traditional notions of quality management with the need to build participatory forms of assessment, delivery and evaluation.

Whether based on ideas of quality or research, it was argued that evaluation processes should provide structured opportunities to bring together people to discuss, reflect on and debate particular services, problems or occurrences (Jones and Leverett 2008). Contemporary approaches sought to embrace ideas from systems theory that focused on the needs of the customer, highlighted the continuous nature of change and perceived change to be the collective responsibility of all staff. These approaches encouraged a shift from deficit models (e.g. based on individual performance/problems) to those that focused on systems as culturally open, welcoming, questioning and learning spaces (Oakland 1993; Locock 2001; McIver 2002).

It was argued that rather than performance indicators, external evaluators and inspectors needed to have better knowledge management systems that were created by workers and that collected, analysed and stored information about the types and frequency of demand that came from service users (Seddon 2008). In particular, multi-professional managers were encouraged to examine how staff met demand, how much capacity the organisation had to respond to demand, how well (from the service users' point of view) the organisation met demand and what major steps were needed to meet demand (e.g. did different service users require the organisation to do different things) (Seddon 2008).

This systemic form of analysis emerged in literature on family support that suggested knowledge networks (involving children, parents, families and communities) should be developed to foster multi-professional and integrated working (Dolan 2006b; Pinkerton 2006). In particular practitioners were encouraged to pose a series of questions including:

- Who was the service user (e.g. parents, young children, children, young people, older people community members)?

- What major activities were they seeking (e.g. home visits, play provision, schooling, youth services, parenting support, counselling, family therapy, residential care, transport, etc.)?

- What was the purpose of the work (e.g. development, protection, compensation, redistribution, etc.)?

- What methods were married with service user expectations (e.g. empathy, advocacy/self-advocacy, community development, peer support, etc.)?

- What level of work was involved (e.g. open access, targeted single-service support, targeted multi-agency intervention or acute intervention)?

- Which professionals were required to work with the service users (e.g. social worker, family worker, psychologist, community worker, youth worker, voluntary sector worker, etc.)?

(Pinkerton 2006)

This led to the recommendation that practitioners/service providers evaluate themselves in collaboration with others on the basis of whether they had ensured that services were flexible, promoted engagement with the view of service users, enabled creativity, had drawn from a range of expertise (e.g. professional, service user, family members, friends, neighbours, community members, etc.), recognised cultural diversity and promoted inclusion (Pinkerton 2006; Davis 2011). In Chapter 5 (contemporary management) this approach was connected to notions of process, capacity, method, outcomes and meaning-making (Pinkerton 2006; Dahlberg et al. 2007).

It was argued that the central approach to multi-professional services should involve processes of meaning-making that were interactive, enabled dialogue and involved sensitive listening that acknowledged the prejudices of the different people involved (Dahlberg et al. 2007; Davis 2011). This approach encouraged evaluation to concentrate on analysing complex ideas/problems and different people's views of the same service. It also encouraged joint analysis of everyday problems, methods and decision-making processes (Dahlberg et al. 2007; Davis 2011). The task of evaluation became to help the actors involved develop their critical capacities rather than judge how good or bad a service was (Dahlberg et al. 2007).

Similarly, the role of teaching and learning moved from teaching students objective realities to encouraging people (through supportive frameworks/networks) to expand their ability to think and therefore collaboratively find diverse solutions to the issues they encounter in their workplaces (Seddon 2008; Davis 2011).

In the case of Penwall, the local authority recognised the limitations of the external report and set up a new process that aimed to:

- take a group approach to service development (including connecting learning from family/nurture groups and children/young people's groups) and develop a culture of participation

- develop participatory ways of enabling service users to influence service delivery

- create events that enabled dialogue with children and young people and to develop a local peer support/networking approach led by older young people in the community

- develop formal and participatory groups for young people experiencing additional support linked to the children and young people's partnership.

Penwall service providers worked with a children's rights organisation to redesign their processes. At the centre of this development was the idea that services would be based on collaborative decision-making. A series of 'agenda days' were initially carried out by the children's rights organisations in the local area. Subsequently, young people who experienced additional support were enabled to deliver their own 'agenda days' with other young people. This enabled the local authority to co-construct evaluation processes with children and young people. Key issues identified by the young people were the need to address bullying in schools, the need to improve processes of transition and the need to challenge cultures of labelling.

Moreover, young people were also enabled to develop structures of peer support. In particular a group of young people who had experienced being educated in learning centres led a pupil participation group to develop their own report on the reasons that young people found it difficult to attend school (e.g. labelling, stereotyping, bullying, feeling unsafe, tiredness, anxiety, trauma and stress). They also identified how schools could be improved (particularly contrasting the trusting, supportive, relaxed, participatory, non-judgemental, strengths-based approach of staff/pupils in learning centres to the deficit/labelling approaches of some staff/pupils in schools). The young people found that a key element of the improved provision involved having a flexible timetable, working with adults who took their problems seriously and being in smaller size classes. They put forward suggestions for how learning centres could be improved (e.g. better sports facilities, more creative activities, child care facilities, more outings and a wider range of subjects). They collected parents' views on alternative learning pathways (which were universally positive concerning the way that provision had improved their children's confidence/self-esteem, calmness, approach to education, attainment levels, ability to explore employment routes and feelings of being cared for/appreciated by others) and information on elective home education (finding that young people liked the home educators group and felt the resource should be available more often) and on hospital school (finding that young people wanted more subjects and more time). They also reflected on their own approach to participation and concluded that they could develop on-line approaches to participation and peer support.

The children and young people's views were supported by local online evaluations of schools by pupils and teachers that identified disparities between teachers' and pupils' perspectives of how much shouting, arguments, caring and listening goes on in their schools. In the main teachers rated schools as more positive environments than their pupils.

It was possible to conclude that children and young people's measures of successful service included academic, vocational, social and emotional outcomes. Quality assurance structures at Penwall are framed to analyse input (what is being invested), process (how is provision matched to users), outputs (impact on quantity) and outcomes (impact on quality). Indicators balance learners', parents' and staff/managers' outcomes (e.g. concerning progress/achievement, assessment by staff, ability to have views on learning heard, ability to take responsibility for learning, development of collaborative decision-making, existence of learner plans, variety of learning formats, suitability of learning materials, equality of access to the curriculum, prevention of discrimination, knowledge/training of teachers and provision of appropriate support). It was clear from the available data that a significant minority of pupils had failed to experience quality learning at specific times in their schooling. It was also clear that their specific experiences were contrary to the aims and policies of the authority and schools.

The young people developed a video on their findings and reported them to senior managers/officers at a presentation event. There was discussion at the event about how to improve mainstream schools in order that pupils did not have to leave mainstream provision and attend learning centres. In particular the young people were keen for teachers to adopt more relational approaches to working with pupils and for class sizes to be reduced.

Senior authority managers welcomed the report and agreed that schools should become more relational and inclusive. However, they also voiced awareness that resource barriers could prevent change in mainstream schools and asked for more in-depth research and planning to be carried out with schools to enable more precise strategies for change to be developed. Such local strategies already exist and schools in Penwall had developed a variety of approaches to improve issues of well-being (e.g. circle time, collaborative group working, celebration assemblies, small group learning, paired/ peer working, residential learning events, holistic positive-ethos curriculum, behaviour polices, improved staff training and playground redesign). It was possible to conclude that there was a gap between the staff, children and young people's aspirations for improved learning environments and the reality that pupils experienced on the ground. However, it should be noted that Penwall was in the early stages of its new policies and that the senior managers were keen to bridge this gap by further developing the collaborative and participatory nature of their evaluation processes.

In particular we would recommend that in the next stages of their development they check the extent to which strategies for making schools more pupil friendly (e.g. circle time and behaviour policies) are actually based on suggestions made by children and young people. We are aware that such tools are only as good as the people who use them and, as Seddon (2008) teaches us, there is a potential for such approaches to involve top-down decision-making when it comes to solutions rather than enabling solutions to be collaboratively developed.

In Chapter 3 (participation) we argued that it is important when developing collaborative approaches to attend to the politics of group work and develop flexible approaches that enable different characters with different backgrounds to be involved (Bolton 2010). Managers in Penwall's inclusion services had certainly enabled a range of children and young people to take leadership roles in their evaluation processes. They now have a strong grasp of the issues that concern children and young people. The next stage for Penwall is to continue to support the leadership abilities of these children and young people and work out strategies for how to speed up processes of participation, evaluation and change that enable solutions to be developed collaboratively and schools to actually become more equitable spaces. This has enabled us to conclude that there can be no one perfect way to 'do' evaluation, that there is a need to balance different methods/measurements of analysis with various structures for change and, therefore, that evaluation is a process and not an event.

 Activity

In light of this chapter and Chapter 3 (participation) can you consider an evaluation that you have carried out? Would you plan it differently? Could you return to the Table 6.2 on multi-professional evaluation and use the indicators of a social model approach to critique your own approach? Can you discuss the concept of collaborative evaluation with your colleagues and service providers? Do you enable community members to participate in evaluations? What plans and processes do you use to ensure your evaluation has local meaning?

Conclusion

This chapter has argued that approaches such as total quality management and research-based evaluation are problematic because they are not sufficiently participatory, impose objective measures and put too much reliance on outsiders who do not have an understanding of local contexts. It utilised the case study from Penwall to encourage you to move towards more relational approaches to evaluation. In particular it demonstrated that problems occur when the focus of evaluation is concerned with impairment and not the barriers that disabled children encounter in their lives. It compared such problems to critiques of quality management and encouraged you to develop group, interrelation and collaborative evaluation processes.

In essence we have promoted a collective approach to multi-professional evaluation that does not separate out service users, practitioners, managers, external experts and community members and does not locate itself in one service. In so doing, we have encouraged you to think of evaluation as a long-term, well planned and interactive process that seeks to better understand meaning rather than use apparently objective measures to apportion blame.

Recommended further reading

Bolton, G. (2010) *Reflective Practice: Writing and Professional Development*. London: Sage.

Boyne, G. A. (2003) 'Sources of public service improvement: a critical review and research agenda', *Journal of Public Administration Research and Theory*, 13 (4): 767–94.

Dolan, P., Canavan, J. and Pinkerton, J. (eds) (2006) *Family Support as Reflective Practice*. London: Jessica Kingsley.

7

Multi-professional learning and creativity

Chapter Overview

Chapter 4 (traditional management) demonstrated that issues of multi-professional hierarchies can create barriers in multi-professional services. Chapter 5 suggested that leadership in your workplace could be provided by a range of people irrespective of personal cultures, professional backgrounds and managerial positions. It concluded that change processes should involve collective reflexivity that recognises the diverse perspectives of those involved in multi-disciplinary services. This chapter builds on such ideas by considering the concepts, environments and relationships that stimulate creative, collaborative and innovative learning. It specifically draws from the findings of a collaborative European research project (CREANOVA) that identified a number of individual, structural and relational aspects of creativity and innovation to conclude that the environments that best promote multi-professional creativity and innovation involve supportive frameworks, value cross-cultural professional interaction and balance ideas of autonomy, diversity and collective working.

Case Study CREANOVA Project: multi-professional learning

CREANOVA was a major EU research project (funded under the Transversal Research element of the Lifelong Learning Programme, European Commission Project No. 143725-LLP-1-2008-1-ES-KA1-KA1SCR). The project involved universities, regional governments and learning-design specialists in a process of research, experimentation and analysis that investigated the role and nature of innovation and creativity in European society. The project examined how learning situations and processes could be constructed in the creative and technology industries to achieve sustainable innovation. This case study is utilised in this chapter to demonstrate the individual, structural and relation issues that promote creative and innovative multi-professional working.

The Scottish CREANOVA team compared project findings concerning the creative and technology sectors to multi-professional learning in the social care sector (Farrier et al. 2011). In particular it considered ideas concerning multi-professional creativity and innovation that emerged from the evaluation of a mentoring course (McNicoll et al. 2010; Brady et al. 2010) that had been carried out in the social care sector (over two academic semesters) by staff from the University of Edinburgh School of Education in collaboration with the Coalition of Childcare Organisations, the Scottish Social Services Council and the Scottish Government. The course had been set up to enable contrasting professionals in the childcare sector to come together, share ideas about mentoring and develop national guidance for their sector.

Concepts of multi-professional learning, innovation and creativity?

Davis and Hughes (2005) found that professionals in integrated settings wanted more learning opportunities. Many writers have highlighted learning as key to processes of multi-professional working (Marks 1994; Leathard 2003; Milne 2005; Scott 2006; Stone and Rixon 2008; Munroe 2011). In particular, it has been suggested that there needs to be a systemic shift from compliance to learning cultures in multi-professional children and family services and that local authorities who have made this shift have done so in spite of rather than because of ideas of regulation/standardisation (Munroe 2011). The CREANOVA project utilised a range of methods to investigate multi-professional learning including analysis of case study learning projects, a statistical survey of staff in organisations and qualitative interviews of leaders of innovative processes (interviews were carried out with 50 leaders of creative/innovative public, voluntary and private sector companies in the Basque Country, Scotland, Estonia and Finland) (Farrier et al. 2011).

This section of the chapter connects the summary findings of the project to conceptual ideas concerning individual, group and interactive learning. It utilises specific findings from the mentoring project to consider how learning can stimulate innovative practice, enable creative interaction and foster work-based change. For example, the CREANOVA project found that people defined creativity and innovation in a range of ways including the following:

- Innovation is an ongoing practical, technological, group-led activity aimed at optimising, updating and replacing objects, processes and outcomes that is driven by need.

- Creativity is a finite, limited and soft process, event or moment that generates unusual individual or collective ideas that bring something new into the world (materialise need) but not always for a useful end outcome.

- Creativity happens before or is a prerequisite for innovation and/or innovation is creativity with targets.

- Creativity and innovation are the same thing involving a connection between practical and educational experience and personal confidence, curiosity and enthusiasm.

(Farrier et al. 2011)

Creativity was often defined as the production of new, novel and useful ideas or knowledge (Mumford and Gustafson 1998; Woodman et al. 1993; Ibáñez et al. 2010). The CREANOVA respondents' definitions at first appeared contradictory, for example when they suggested creativity and innovation were the same thing or alternatively that one came before the other (Farrier et al. 2011; Davis et al. 2011). It was possible from participants' responses to broaden our definition of creativity that suggested it was any act, idea or product that changed an existing situation (Csikszentmihalyi 1996) to suggest that creativity and innovation were similar activities but that innovation was a process that involved creativity.

Many respondents confirmed West's (2002) suggestion that creativity occurs primarily at the early stages of innovation processes with innovation and implementation coming later, innovation being perceived as the adaptation, adoption or implementation of novel and useful ideas, products or processes (Kanter 1988; Van de Ven 1986; Ibáñez et al. 2010).

Individual and group concepts of learning and creativity

Chapter 5 (contemporary management) recommended that you utilise reflexivity on a daily basis to question your practices, beliefs and concepts and examine whether your work took account of the views of others. It suggested that reflexive practice was an essential part of the work of the professional (Schön 1987; Brookfield 1995). In Chapter 2 (assessment) we suggested that conceptual clarity is difficult to establish in fast-moving work roles and that you needed to be proactive in combining processes of assessment, thinking and action. We suggested that professionals needed to feel confident to make decisions, share information and start processes of dialogue in their workplace.

The concept of reflexivity as an activity for individuals can be connected with individualist ideas concerning learning. Such ideas were heavily influenced by Piagetian concepts concerning cognitive development (Piaget 1975). In particular the achievement of age and stage developmental milestones was attached to notions of normality and difference (Woodhead 2009). These ideas led to the notion that some people learned faster than others and therefore were more able, analytical and advanced. We can see these ideas in the way that proponents of reflexivity separate out the student professional from the qualified/experienced professional (Rice 2007). For example, theories of reflexive learning generally argue that the learner has to be afforded opportunities to engage, reflect, debate and experience self-doubt in order that they become 'self-actualised' where they experience success as the learner and this in turn improves practice (Rice 2007).

Similarly, individualist ideas of self-actualisation have also been used to suggest that creativity is an individual activity carried out by 'special' individuals (Piirto 2004). For example, some respondents in the CREANOVA project connected creativity to issues of talent, cognition, emotion, imagination, genius, insight, introversion, intuition, naivety, openness to experience, over-excitability, passion, perceptiveness, perfectionism, persistence, resilience, risk-taking, self-discipline, self-efficacy, tolerance for ambiguity and volition or will. However, they also argued that cognition and genius on their own were not enough to enable creative ideas to become innovative processes or products (Cropley and Cropley 2009; Ibáñez et al. 2010). These respondents connected ideas of teaching and learning.

Theories of teaching and learning (e.g. with communities, adults and children) have seen a shift across a range of ideas from the following:

• Formal notions of conditioning that suggested that people learnt from repetition, reward and punishment (Laird 1985). These can be connected to the top-down management ideas discussed in Chapter 4 (traditional management) that assumed, for example, that workers needed extrinsic rewards (Seddon 2008).

• Constructivist ideas (e.g. Vygotsky 1995) that built on the notion that the child/adult should be enabled to be an active learner and the teacher should start from the learner's everyday understanding when trying to transmit knowledge (Dahlberg et al. 1999). Social-constructivists recognised the learner's ability to make choices/meanings and therefore to make alternative constructions of the knowledge of the teacher (Dahlberg et al. 1999).

• Group approaches to reflexive learning that highlighted the connections between learning, environment, experience and reflection (Dewey 1938; Kolb 1984). These approaches highlighted the potential for group learning, peer learning and mentoring to involve flat hierarchies (Turnbull 2009).

• More political ideas concerning learning that outlined the connection between dialogue, respect and the lived experience (Freire 1970).

We can unpack these ideas in relation to concepts of mentoring. Professional guidance in social care has differentiated between different models of mentoring (e.g. a one-to-one shared partnership model, a peer group model, a team model, a group model and a single organisational model (CCUO 2011)). One-to-one mentoring was perceived to facilitate significant transitions in knowledge, work or thinking (Megginson and Clutterbuck 1995: 13), to foster supportive dialogue (Garvey and Galloway 2002) and to help the learner develop their skills, improve performance and become 'the person they want to be' (Parsloe 2009: 1).

In the case of the mentoring project the CCUO adapted the frameworks of their organisations based on their learning and developed national guidance for mentoring. Analysis of concepts of group reflexivity, change and anti-hierarchy established in the mentoring course encouraged the learners to sensitively produce guidance that aimed to avoid being overly prescriptive, tried to establish different versions of mentoring and encouraged choice when planning organisational strategies. The learners were encouraged to put into practice ideas from academic literature on mentoring about avoiding hierarchies, promoting learner-led discussions/goal setting and enabling mentee choice/self-direction (McNicoll et al. 2010).

Some authors have argued that training for staff involved in public services has became too functional and knowledge has become 'standardized and routinized' (MacDonald 1995: 3). They have suggested that as competence models have become more prevalent in education and training, knowledge has become impoverished:

> Learners and teachers are denied the opportunity to develop
> an orientation towards understanding a given social problem
> rather than achieving technical success. (Ozga 2000: 57)

Formal approaches to mentoring have particularly been applied to new staff that have to fulfil an induction period (McKimm et al. 2007). For example, in Scotland teachers are required to fulfil a formal post-qualification induction year in which they are supported to grow into the profession. Such concepts of mentoring involve a tension between aims that are functional (the expectation that there will be improvements in the performance of the learner) and aspirational (the mentee defines and fulfils their own agenda) (Garvey et al. 2009: 11).

The political context of such learning was analysed by Freire (1970) who made connections between learning, hope and social change. In adult learning the humanistic notion of learner facilitators (who utilised ideas of trust, empathy and relationship building) emerged that questioned the power relations in learning encounters (Rogers and Freiberg 1993). This also led writers in childhood studies to question the assumption that the child should always be the learner and the adult the facilitator. Such approaches encouraged us to recognise that children could learn from as well as help adults learn and that an interaction between different people would involve an interplay of learning and expertise (Mayall 2000). These ideas connect with the argument in Chapter 3 (participation) that participatory processes should be built on the idea that children, families, communities and professionals all have different yet relevant types of expertise that can be utilised to analyse the appropriateness of multi-professional services.

The CREANOVA study found that the mentoring course enabled learners to utilise knowledge from academic learning to become much more proactive in their consideration of their wider task (which was to develop guidelines for the sector) (Farrier et al. 2011). Thus learners approached the establishment of the guidance in creative and flexible ways, were open to new ideas from academics but also tried to build on their own existing knowledge and experience which tended to favour non-hierarchical approaches to mentoring. Within this context participants in the mentoring course did not feel that they had to comply with academic conventions. That is, the process enabled them to reject, adapt and transform the ideas of big thinkers in the field of reflexivity, mentoring, organisational change, learning cycles, etc.

By analysing and comparing the mentoring course to other case studies in the CREANOVA project it became possible to conclude that creativity stemmed from individual and collective processes that involved divergent and convergent thinking and that the mentoring course itself facilitated not just creative thinking but innovative application of that thinking, e.g. when ideas from course discussions were implemented in the workplace (Farrier et al. 2011). Learners particularly highlighted the creative value of working with a range of people who had different types of experience. They suggested that the process generated synthetic, analytical and practical thinking that could be applied to examples from different learners' socio-cultural contexts (e.g. rural training provider organisations, national child care organisations, local authority child care partnerships, etc.).

The course participants included in their final mentoring guidance document advice on formal/informal processes, descriptions of different types of mentoring structures (peer, single-organisation, intra-/inter-organisational) and illustrations of the key aspects of relationship building (planning meetings, keeping notes, agreeing agendas, focusing on mentee's aims, etc.). As such, the document did not nationally prescribe an approach but rather offered a number of processes including key questions that managers/practitioners could follow to help their thinking/discussions if they were debating setting up mentoring processes. The guidance was flexible but did suggest that formal approaches to mentoring may be more sustainable than informal approaches.

The findings of the mentoring evaluation substantiated theories on education, intelligence, creativity and innovation that have encouraged us to think of learning as a combination of the individual (e.g. psychological/philosophical), social (e.g. interactive), experiential (e.g. long-term) and environmental (e.g. ability to work freely without oppression) (Ibáñez et al. 2010).

Woodhead (2009) encouraged us to reject crude versions of learning and developmentalism that are based on rigid hierarchies and to engage with more contemporary approaches to development that connect the physical, relational and cultural to changes in growth, learning and well-being. Such ideas have been put forward in disability studies by people who have attempted to move beyond the social model of disabilities emphasis on structural barriers (Davis and Watson 2002). These writers have argued that individual, biological, social and cultural issues are interconnected in learning environments where experiences of hierarchy and discrimination become embodied in the learner and that the learner's reactions to the subsequent learning experience cannot be neatly disassociated from any of these factors (Davis and Watson 2002).

The mentoring course involved a combination of academic ideas on learning and practical activities. The participants were particularly critical of sessions where they could not easily connect academic ideas to their practical experience. Indeed, the full meaning and relevance of specific academic ideas only became apparent in the second half of the course when the participants started to develop the national guidance, that is, when the use of academic ideas became more of an embodied experience.

Sternberg (2003) argued that the skill of creativity is not enough on its own to stimulate innovation and that to stimulate innovation one had to *use* the skill of creativity. It was possible to advance this idea using the findings of the CREANOVA project to state that the skill, knowledge, values and experience of creativity is not enough to stimulate creativity and innovation if the spaces that learners and workers live in are so formally structured or conceptually limited that they do not meet people's aspirations to practically utilise their skills, knowledge, values and experiences (Farrier et al. 2011).

The CREANOVA project found a need for learning processes to connect theory and practice and therefore to balance autonomy, freedom and guidance/frameworks. The participants on the mentoring course were particularly keen to take responsibility for their own learning (in keeping with Scardamalia and Bereiter 2006) but they also saw the benefits of balancing individual, peer and lecturer/tutor-framed learning.

The CREANOVA findings supported the contention that learning embedded in an emergent activity can enable a qualitative transformation of the entire activity system (Engeström 2004). For example, the participants in the mentoring course were very verbal when they did not feel the context of learning was appropriate. They viewed the university lecturers as facilitators who were no more or less important to the process of learning than themselves (we can contrast this perception with the apparently 'expert' role of external evaluators in Chapter 6) and the evaluation indicated that they learnt more relevantly from practical group collaborative sessions than from lecturer-led moments. This interactive process enabled the participants to bring together disparate ideas to formulate new strategies for mentoring within their own organisations.

Carpenter and Dickinson (2008) differentiate between different types of learning including:

- shared/multi-professional learning where two professionals learn in parallel/side by side about a subject

- inter-professional where professionals learn about each other

- trans-professional where learning crosses or merges boundaries and common learning (where professional learning follows a common curriculum).

They drew on Barr (1996) to differentiate between learning that is part of a qualification, a discrete module, a work base/place, a college/ university or was pre-/post-qualifying. They also contrasted learning that involved different types of assessment (e.g. group or individual), delivery (e.g. interactive/didactic) and time lengths (e.g. short course vs. long-term qualification). The mentoring course involved continuous, shared, inter- and intra-professional development that did not lead to a specific qualification. The course was specifically designed for the participants with the aim of enabling them to reflect on their own organisational strategies. The course utilised a range of methods including face-to-face events, scenario-based learning, online learning and virtual classrooms. The participants especially valued the opportunity to interact with each other in face-to-face classes that had a practical focus.

It has been argued that multi-professional learning should utilise such approaches to joint training to enable professionals to focus on specific issues within integrated working (e.g. roles, duties, structures, relationships and concepts), break down professional barriers and develop comparative/collaborative perspectives (Carpenter and Dickinson 2008; Davis 2011). It has been suggested that such learning opportunities should also be utilised as a complementary activity with other approaches that foster more integrated perspectives such as joint problem-solving, developing shared goals, having regular meetings and trust-building activities (Bertram et al. 2002; Gilbert and Bainbridge 2003; Leathard 2003b; Tomlinson 2003; Harker et al. 2004; Frost 2005; Milne 2005; Anning et al. 2006; Scott 2006; Fitzgerald and Kay 2008; Glenny and Roaf 2008; Stone and Rixon 2008; Walker 2008).

Such approaches can be contrasted with the hierarchical idea of formal functional training. For example, we had no idea at the start of the mentoring course how the journey would end up. It resulted in a successful outcome because the participants were enabled to take power over the process, to interact on an equal basis with other participants/ the lecturers and to develop creative ideas that were dropped into a more formal process of innovation (the task of developing a guidance document for their sector, the Scottish Government and Scottish Social Services Council).

Redefining creativity and innovation

This enabled us to redefine creativity and innovation to say that they are similar (e.g. both involve change) but that creativity is an individual or shared embodied process including the moments, ideas or thoughts that begin a process of innovation and that innovation is the embodied and embedded process that brings together creative output in a way that specifically leads to the transformation or adaptation of an existing entity, object or process.

This finding was problematic for the idea of creative personal ability (Piirto 2004). Creativity may often be individual (arising from the confluence of knowledge, creative thinking and motivation) (Adams 2005) but also arises from and can be stimulated by interaction. The CREANOVA project findings confirmed the view of Csikszentmihalyi (1996) that creativity does not happen simply inside people's heads, but in the interaction between a person's thoughts and socio-cultural contexts. The evaluation of the mentoring project found (in keeping with Mumford 2002; Mulgan et al. 2007; Ibáñez et al. 2010) that creative ideas and the thinking behind them are only useful if they can provide new processes, revolutionise approaches in an area or be fitted into, adapted to or employed in existing processes.

 Activity

Can you consider your own formal and informal learning experiences? Did/do they involve transmission (top-down), peer, facilitated or group learning? What approaches do you value? Have you experience of working through academic ideas, with practical multi-professional groupings? Did/does your professional training/ qualification involve creative workshops on multi-professional learning with professionals from other agencies/sectors? How interactive are they? In the case of the mentoring course the participants interacted in a very collaborative manner – has that been the case in your experience? Is there anything that you, your colleagues (if you are a student) your lecturers could do to ensure that joint learning opportunities are available, relevant, collaborative and interactive?

Environments for innovation, creativity and change

The mentoring course evaluation found that students relished the shift to more reciprocal, interactive and dialogic learning and greatly appreciated the opportunity to work with colleagues in spaces that overcame hierarchy, enabled trust and fostered joint working (McNicoll 2010). For example, many participants emphasised how group processes enabled them to stimulate their own individual creativity. It has been argued that multi-professional integrated services require common aims, language, values and principles (Hannon et al. 2005). However, in Chapter 5 we indicated that collective reflexivity did not require professionals to subscribe to one way of thinking; it should involve respect for diverse ideas and enable open dialogue concerning the pros and cons of different approaches. In particular, this was related to the development of local multi-professional forums (that discuss issues of assessment, planning and delivery). The participants in the mentoring course had a range of professional backgrounds (including coming from the public, private and voluntary sectors), yet participants were willing to consider different approaches to mentoring and to develop guidance that was not overly prescriptive.

They did not subsume all their identities into a single position but rather worked on understanding how each other's ideas concerning learning and mentoring related to and would impact on their different organisational contexts.

Therefore the notion of 'common language' in multi-professional settings is problematic, not least because it overlooks the politics of such settings. For example, the merger of care and education services in Sweden resulted in non-teachers being subsumed by teaching cultures and subsequent schoolification of early years and day/out-of-school care (Moss and Bennett 2006; Cohen et al. 2004). We can connect here to the conclusions of Chapter 4 (traditional management) and Chapter 6 (evaluation) that multi-professional working should value diversity to argue (in keeping with Chapter 5) that the development of common flexible processes is a more appropriate basis for multi-professional working than a common language unless the common language enshrines an acceptance of diverse perspectives and practices.

Collaborative environments

The CREANOVA project found that informal and formal learning aided the development of individual and organisational diversity, innovation and creativity. In particular participants in the mentoring course suggested that there was much to be gained from innovative learning processes that connected learning to practical contexts, were embedded in everyday existing processes, promoted interactive group work and enabled cooperation between different level staff (McNicoll 2010). Respondents related their need for creativity/innovation to a range of individual, group, organisational and environmental issues including:

- change in the environment, e.g. customer demand, environmental conditions, rules on safety, new technology, social/cultural values, competition and market data

- improvement and efficiency processes

- things in one's individual self-view, goals and values

- the wish to have new, different, contrasting and divergent ideas, products and processes

- the necessity for long-term, integrated or universal products or approaches

- processes that attempted to overcome failure and develop security (e.g. financial, social and ecological security).

Respondents argued that the individual and collective need to solve different problems stimulated a necessity for creativity (in keeping with Ibáñez et al. 2010). The CREANOVA findings substantiate Unsworth's (2001) argument that creativity is a response to present or expected internal drivers (e.g. the mentoring course members needed to develop guidance relevant to themselves) and external drivers (the mentoring course members had to respond to the request to develop national guidance for the sector and an expectation that an appropriate document would be delivered on time).

Some writers have related creative/innovative diversity and dynamism to the need to overcome a variety of pressures (Schumpeter 1934; Amabile 1996; Ibáñez et al. 2010). Such drivers have also been related to a need to overcome economic and social problems (Schumpeter 1934 Fagerberg 2003; Mouleart et al. 2005; Mulgan 2006). In the case of the mentoring course the development was required to be relevant to a sector that involved professionals who had moved from social work, teaching, childhood practice, community work, nursing, etc. The sector also involved workers from a whole spectrum of backgrounds across Scotland. Hence, the need for creative and innovative guidance was perceived to come from environmental, socio-cultural, professional, governmental, and economic issues. For example, many providers were working to tight budgets in small organisations that may not be able to self-finance or organise a complex mentoring scheme but could perhaps be encouraged to develop local/regional collaborations with other organisations.

This finding enabled us to expand the view that everyday creativity involved coping with continuously changing local environments (Amabile 1996; Richards 2007) to suggest that creativity and innovation is a response to continuous change at different levels (e.g. local, regional, national and international), of different types (individual, team, community, network, organisational, cultural, societal) and of different timescales (short, intermediate and long term). This finding also confirmed the view set out in Chapters 3, 4 and 5 that multi-professional working involves unavoidable continuous change, that the need for innovation should consider issues of capacity and that therefore we need to base our ideas for change on a collective, complex and systemic analysis of what is actually possible for any individual, team, community or organisation.

Creativity, innovation and freedom

Chapter 4 (traditional management) and Chapter 5 (contemporary management) suggested that we had to balance out notions of standardisation, hierarchy, collaboration, diversity and flexibility when developing multi-professional working. In particular, Chapter 5 highlighted a tension between writers who sought consensus and the need to provide children and families with flexible services. The CREANOVA project found that respondents related their capacity for creativity/innovation to environmental, individual, group and organisational notions of freedom including:

- individual analysis, collective thinking, power, respect, acceptance, equality, responsibility, experimentation and autonomy

- the need for flat hierarchies

- flexible, sympathetic and non-judgemental frameworks, relationships, structures and rules

- freedom to express feelings, emotions, love and inspiration

- internationalisation, valuing diversity and cultural exchange/ understanding.

The CREANOVA study findings substantiated writing that has suggested that respondents value being able to work together in environments that aim to be creative and innovate for the common good (Etzioni 1993; Ibáñez et al. 2010) and that creativity and innovation did not require complete freedom or laissez-faire approaches in a neo-liberal sense. Interestingly, a number of respondents pointed out that too much freedom could be problematic if it prevented creative ideas from coming to fruition. They suggested there was a need to balance concepts of freedom with ideas concerning flexible design, process and frameworks. For example, one respondent in the CREANOVA study had been involved in utilising a computer program to enable young people in residential care to co-design their home. The project aimed to be participatory but had to balance out issues of creative design with framework issues concerning budgets, planning and health/safety. Here creativity and innovation involve concepts of freedom that flattened the hierarchy between designers and residents but it did not involve a complete lack of frameworks.

The CREANOVA study therefore confirmed the suggestion that freedom and environment are connected and that creative and innovatory practices do not occur in an abstract vacuum (Ibáñez et al. 2010). The findings also substantiated the critique of hierarchy established in Chapter 4 (traditional management) and connected with the work of writers who have argued that creativity and innovation are hindered by techniques of hierarchy, simplification, uniformity and control associated with the traditional industrial era (Miller 2003).

Ideas of freedom were connected by respondents in the CREANOVA project to a range of softer human relational issues. Creativity and innovation was believed to benefit from environments that cultivated vision, imagination, aesthetic awareness, spiritual sensitivity, gentleness, generosity, caring, compassion and a recognition of what is loving and life-affirming in the human soul (in keeping with Goodlad 1997: 125; Ibáñez et al. 2010). This finding substantiated writing that suggests creativity and innovation involves issues of health and well-being, personal growth and development (Richards 2007), the evolution of cultural awareness (Richards 2007) and notions of emotional understanding, bounce-back-ability, diverse learning and cultural variety (Hargreaves 2003; Ibáñez et al. 2010).

This finding confirmed those of Chapter 5 that suggested we needed to balance the development of common multi-professional structures, processes and spaces (such as the Pentesk teams/forums) with processes that question the power relations within organisations and enable service users and frontline staff to set organisational agendas.

Creativity, innovation and environment

Respondents were particularly concerned about the restrictive nature of conservative and hierarchical environments, arguing that environments:

- should be friendly, fun, creative, keen, eager, proactive, confident, stimulating, liberating, permissive, energetic, empathetic, tolerant, ego-free, courageous, fear-free, tolerant, flexible, inspirational, relaxed, supportive, fast-moving, actively listening, emotional and creative

- should have a tradition of innovation, enable people to try new things and think outside the norm

- could be grown by public funding (e.g. involving autonomous regions) and partnership between different local, national, international, public, private and voluntary sectors

- must be information rich (e.g. based on up-to-date research), experienced, knowledgeable, challenging, testing, participatory (e.g. listens to people) and entrepreneurial

- must balance freedom and regulation (e.g. goal orientation, performance, etc.)

- should stimulate interaction, involve exchange (local/international, social and Internet), include dynamic and quiet spaces and involve attractive spaces

- must be characterised by effective leadership that is not overbearing/ hierarchical/bureaucratic and/or hesitant

- involve personal, group, team and organisational motivation and growth that includes role models, mentoring, support and learning.

The CREANOVA findings ask us to question the design and aesthetics of the multi-professional spaces where we meet service users and colleagues. They encourage us to connect to ideas concerning respect and recognition by ensuring that such spaces are welcoming, thoughtful and warm.

Creativity and innovation were thought by some writers to be highly dependent on the connection between issues in environmental systems (helpful frameworks) and the activities of creative individuals and groups (Cropley and Cropley 2009; Ibáñez et al. 2010). The CREANOVA study confirmed Cropley and Cropley's (2009) idea that systems can be discouraging or inhibiting and/or (on the other hand) nurturing, stimulating and inspiring.

The mentoring course became such an environment. The participants were located across Scotland but they utilised the university's virtual learning spaces, skype and telephone conversations to generate and exchange ideas. It was possible to conclude in keeping with (Cropley and Cropley 2009) that innovation and creativity during the mentoring process benefited from the flexible distribution of roles, themes and problems and the sharing of activities, joint learning and joint responsibility. The mentoring course engendered a 'creativogenic' climate (Cropley and Cropley 2009) that embraced the concept of open learning as well as provided social environments to stretch individuals. This climate involved cooperation between public, private and voluntary organisations.

Individual course members acted autonomously and collectively and had the opportunity to work on their own, with peers or in groups (Sternberg 2003, 2007; Cropley and Cropley 2009). The most impressive aspect of the group dynamics of the course was tolerance (acceptance of difference, openness of variability and absence of rigid sanctions against mistakes) (Cropley and Cropley 2009). Despite their diverse backgrounds course members provided peer support, gave encouragement and accepted non-conformist behaviour. This enabled the range of participants' views to be heard and original ideas to emerge. This finding reinforced our ideas set out in Chapter 5 (contemporary management) that multi-professional working is fostered by environments that embrace diversity.

It has been suggested that creativity and innovation develop in atmospheres that are free from anxiety, avoid time pressures and enable sensible risk-taking (Cropley and Cropley 2009). It would be fair to say that the participants in the mentoring process actually felt anxious (occasionally) about whether they could meet their deadline for publication of the guidance and that at times this pressure actually acted as a stimulus. However, overall the CREANOVA respondents confirmed Cropley and Cropley's (2009) ideas that emotional comfort is connected to physical and cultural comfort.

Ibáñez et al. (2010) (drawing on Sternberg 2003) highlighted the need for motivation, stickability, resilience and personality. This raised specific questions about individual, professional and group resilience. Resilience was defined by respondents as relating to both individual and group processes. The participants in the mentoring course utilised collective dialogue and support as a resource from which to fuel their resilience in a way that combined emotional strength, physical stamina and sense of humour. This again suggested that innovation and creativity involve an embodied process where people's ways of being are affected by the issues around them. In relation to multi-professional working this pointed to the need to not simply involve service users and colleagues in collaborative discussions but also to create spaces that are welcoming, supportive and resilient on different levels (emotional, aesthetic, cultural, strategic and physical).

 Activity

What types of environments do you work in? Take a look round the places you work – are they welcoming to visitors? Do you have physical meeting spaces that are aesthetically pleasing? Are there spaces for one-to-one meetings, group meetings, noisy meetings, etc.? How formal are the rules where you work? Are rules applied in a hierarchical way? Can you identify rules/frameworks that hinder or help multi-professional working? To what extent are you able to develop collaborative and innovative ideas, processes and outcomes with service users, community members and colleagues?

Multi-professional creativity, innovation and interaction

It has been argued that innovation and creativity are connected to social, cultural and economic interaction (West 2002). Just as this book has stressed the need for multi-professional collaboration the CREANOVA study found that interaction was a crucial aspect of creativity and innovation. Respondents suggested that interaction:

- stimulated innovation and creativity within and between public, voluntary and private companies, departments, networks, clusters, peers, colleagues, groups, sectors and organisations

- could involve a mixture of people with different specialisms, professional backgrounds, expertise, qualifications, learning, experience, etc.

- needed to be empathetic, trustful, honest, loving, accepting, open, clear, transparent, culturally aware and respectful

- needed to include joint thinking and action

- was related to supportive relationships and hierarchies that included feedback, evaluation, strategic coordination and development

- was prohibited by formality and confidentiality

- was connected with international, regional and national communication, exhibitions, exchange, outsourcing, participatory collaboration and job-sharing

- was connected with the need to balance personal versus collective goals and involved personal attributes such as reflexivity, active listening skills, a willingness to take risks, a lack of ego, open minds and the ability to go beyond traditional thinking.

Respondents suggested (in keeping with West 2002; Ibáñez et al. 2010) that there were great benefits to be gained from processes that synthesised research and theory to advance our understanding in the workplace. Similarly, many respondents echoed the view that the speed of change could be accelerated by international cooperation, inter-firm collaboration, industrial networks and cross specialism working (Schienstock and Hämäläinen 2001; Mumford 2002; Tuomi 2002; SITRA 2005; Hämäläinen 2005; Bruce 2009; Ibáñez et al. 2010). Respondents believed (in keeping with Cropley and Cropley 2009; Ibáñez et al. 2010) that innovation and creativity benefited from flexibility, inter-disciplinarity and cross-fertilisation of ideas at managerial and front-line levels and that collaboration with academic and sector centres greatly increased their knowledge and expertise.

The CREANOVA project found that cross-sector working was on the increase and that smaller businesses in the private sector could gain a great deal when connected to other organisations by regional centres. The project pointed to the benefits of local, national and international interactive processes that involved employees from different organisations interacting in formal and informal learning spaces (e.g. conferences, seminars, events, workshops, etc.). In a similar way to the mentoring project respondents argued that collaborative exchange, learning by doing, joint problem-solving and shared critical observation fostered innovation and creativity. Leaders and managers in organisations were particularly keen that they and their colleagues should have access to academic and practical knowledge from up-to-date research. In particular, they highlighted the benefits of developing and learning from other people's prototypes. These findings connect with the idea that learning should balance academic and practical tasks (Pascarella and Terenzini 2005; Ibáñez et al. 2010) and that learning can involve exchange within or between communities, disciplines, organisations, job roles or educational institutions (Carneiro 2007; Ibáñez et al. 2010).

The CREANOVA study and the evaluation of the mentoring project confirmed the idea that one of the strongest potential sources available for learning and improvement are people and partnerships outwith an organisation (OECD 2001; Hargreaves 2003; CEDEFOP 2008; Ibáñez et al. 2010; Farrier et al. 2011). In particular respondents highlighted the benefits of community, local, regional, national and international learning centres and networks (Apple and Beane 1995; Jaussi 2002; Ibáñez et al. 2010). A number of respondents (in keeping with writers such as Rogoff 1993; Vygotsky 1995; Bruner 2000; Wells 2001; European Commission 2006; CEDEFOP 2008; Ibáñez et al. 2010) highlighted the importance of interpersonal attributes and ethical values during learning. In particular they mentioned the need for cultural awareness, mediation, equity and anti-discrimination during internal and external networking. Notions of dialogic, trusting, multidimensional, egalitarian, transformational, expansive and adaptive learning were highly valued (Searle 1980; Freire 1997; Spinosa et al. 1997; Sepúlveda 2001; Searle and Soler 2004; Engeström 2004; Ibáñez et al. 2010). Specifically, respondents stressed the need for learning around creativity and innovation to enable people to go beyond the limitations of their cultural understanding and to visualise other kinds of cultural orientations of a more complex nature that did not previously exist.

For example, a technological company in Italy had created a partnership with an American company who had much greater access to resources for research and design. Small changes developed through this collaboration dramatically increased the relevance of the Italian company's products to consumers. These findings can be connected with notions in cultural-historical activity theory that highlight the need for innovative learning, co-construction and knowledge transfer (Engeström 1987; Engeström and Escalante 1995; Tuomi-Gröhn 2003; Säljö 2003). In particular these ideas connect to the arguments set out in Chapter 3 (participation) that multi-professional working should stimulate collaboration between professionals, service users and community members and the conclusion of Chapter 5 (contemporary management) that systemic approaches should enable interrelation working that values diversity, ambiguity and uncertainty. For example, over time Pentesk forums and teams acted as structures/spaces of joint analysis that ensured multi-professional learning was focused on the requirements of service users.

This leads us to conclude (in a similar way to Glenny and Roaf 2008) that effective multi-professional relationships should enable professionals to adapt to the ideas of children, families and their colleagues. In Chapter 6 (evaluation) we suggested that there were a number of ways to regularly evaluate service provision and that it was important to have a sound basis for decision-making. Writers on creativity and learning argue that creativity involves an interrelationship between diverse expert knowledge, local environments and autonomy worker responsibility (Csikszentmihalyi 1996; Ibáñez et al. 2010; Farrier et al. 2011). In Chapter 2 we concluded that multi-professional working was valuable when practices/processes emphasised early intervention, prevention and working in partnership. Chapter 2 recommended that you look for the diverse strengths within individuals, families and/or community.

It is our conclusion that understandings of diversity require to be built on well thought-out, planned and resourced processes of dialogue and interaction. This conclusion confirms the arguments of a range of authors who have suggested innovation and creativity can be stimulated in learning environments that enable interaction and dialogue (Chomsky 1977, 1988, 2000; Habermas 1987; Cummins 2002; Ibáñez et al. 2010). Some writers have suggested that creativity is domain specific and clusters in certain industries/sectors (Sternberg et al. 2004; Ibáñez et al. 2010). However, our findings suggest that creativity can be found in a variety of sectors and that creativity and innovation flourish when there is collaboration across sectors.

Respondents to the CREANOVA project highlighted the benefits of diversity, interdependency, complexity and participator/user-centred development. Their ideas supported the conclusions of Chapter 3 and 5 that multi-professional planning should be collaborative and that innovation and creativity benefit from interactive/fluid processes that celebrate diversity (Chan Kim and Mauborge 2005; Von Hippel 2005; Bruce 2009; Ibáñez et al. 2010).

The CREANOVA study also suggested that interaction had to be based on tolerance, flexibility, openness and diversity (Cropley and Cropley 2009). At the centre of this discussion was the notion that creativity and innovation benefited from ideas of equality, cultural awareness and interactive social relations (Mumford and Morel 2003; Mouleart et al. 2005; Hämäläinen 2005; Hämäläinen and Haskell 2007; Ibáñez et al. 2010). The concept of rich knowledge and relationships (Cropley and Cropley 2009) was highlighted by most respondents and this connected to the idea that emerged in the mentoring course that creativity is fostered by rich and varied experiences that enable people to see connections/implications and carry out convergent thinking. However, it also confirmed that creativity is also fostered by divergent thinking that involves making remote associations, linking apparently separate fields and forming new understandings (Ibáñez et al. 2010).

A number of respondents referred to collaborative design processes as the glue that connects innovation and creativity. Their ideas can be connected to the views of Unsworth (2001) who has questioned the idea that creativity is a unitary construct and argued that belief in the homogeneity of creativity hinders a fine-tuned analysis of the processes and factors of creativity. In short these findings confirmed the view that for multi-professional working to lead to innovative service delivery it requires service users to be involved in collaborative design. They also enabled us to argue, once again, that the visionary leader notion promoted in 'quality management' approaches to public services has its limitations because it underplays the benefits of collaborative leadership and design.

The evaluation of the mentoring course also suggested that the adoption of new and adaptive ideas requires a process of design (the process of planning the movement from idea to outcome) within the processes of innovation. In the case of the mentoring course we found that creative, design and innovation processes involved both incremental innovation and disruptive innovation (Figuerdo 2009; Ibáñez et al. 2010). In particular, there were times in the mentoring course when there was disjuncture between the lecturer's aims and the participants' aspirations. This required adaptability and change to be agreed by participants and led to more face-to-face sessions being introduced into the course. This finding reinforced the idea that the analysis of conflict and conflicting ideas should be a central aspect of multi-professional working. In particular we would argue that if we connect the findings of the mentoring course to the experiences from Durham and Pentesk we can demonstrate the possibility for organisations to build a more organic, participatory and integrated approach to multi-professional working that views leadership as being the responsibility of all partners within the process and not the privilege of the few.

Activity

Have you experienced interactive learning processes? Can you use the above information to develop a critique of your experiences? What criteria would you use to define effective collaboration? Can you see connections between this chapter, previous discussion of strengths-based approaches and your own experience? Have you had teachers, lecturers or tutors that took a strengths-based approach to you? What do you think led them to do that? Was it individual, cultural, environmental or professional issues, or a mixture of these?

Conclusion

This chapter has suggested that creativity (the production of new ideas) comes to fruition when innovation processes are connected to notions of flexible design. We concluded that creativity is an individual and/or shared embodied moment that requires to be embedded if it is to specifically lead to the transformation and/or adaptation of an existing or new entity, object or process.

It was argued that learning processes benefited from enabling participants to put abstract academic ideas into practice. In addition, they should recognise that participants in multi-professional settings will have diverse forms of experience and expertise and therefore that interactive learning processes and spaces can enable such experience to be harnessed to develop innovative and creative solutions to issues that arise.

This chapter contrasted different approaches to learning to argue that learning involves a combination of individual, social, experiential and environmental issues. The experiences of the mentoring group suggested that we should assume all participants in multi-professional settings are capable of receiving and giving support for learning to others that fosters processes of positive change. This led us to conclude that you should seek to enable multi-professional learning, creativity and innovation at all levels of your work places. We are particularly of the view that professionals who hide their feelings, errors or uncertainties are actually unprofessional and that it is impossible as human beings for us to be perfect machines. In conclusion, we would like you to see our ideas as an inexact and flexible starting point from which to question, challenge and examine your approaches to joint learning because the CREANOVA project has taught us that we should not be over prescriptive.

📖 Recommended further reading

Carpenter, J. and Dickinson, H. (2008) *Inter-professional Education and Training*. Bristol: Policy Press.

Collins, J. (2008) 'Developing positive relationships', in P. Foley and S. Leverett (eds), (2008) *Connecting with Children: Developing Positive Relationships*. Bristol: Policy Press.

Megginson, D. and Clutterbuck, D. (2009) *Techniques for Coaching and Mentoring*. Oxford: Butterworth-Heinemann.

Final conclusions

This book has promoted the idea that multi-professional working is a contested space, that it requires collaborative concepts, structures and relationships and that it needs to avoid under-utilising the diverse ideas of participants (service user, community member, practitioner, leader or manager). At the same time it has encouraged you to be frank about your own limitations, to fully analyse whether the aims of your service meet the aspirations of service users and to develop processes that value uncertainty, conflict and dialogue. We have argued that strong, trusting and thoughtful collaborative multi-professional relationships can act as a stimulus to creative and innovative working. We have suggested that approaches built on practices of distributive leadership and organic development can overcome hierarchical barriers.

At the centre of our position is the idea that we need to be able to openly and fairly analyse the pros and cons of the multi-professional systems within which we work and welcome the continuous nature of change as a source of collaborative inspiration, incentive and motivation. Within this context we have called for you to develop local knowledge networks (learning relationships and structures) that can enable collaborative/embedded evaluation, allow partners to map a range of local problems/solutions, help multi-professional working to understand the expertise of service users, assist us all to examine the capacity of service providers/users and provide firmer ground from which to jointly make decisions about services. This approach specifically encouraged you to question why, how and where you provide services and to examine what services are for (e.g. to enable redistribution, employment, development, rights, recognition or respect).

Our hope is that the book has provided you with a solid basis from which to develop your thinking and will contribute to processes where children, families and communities experience improved life outcomes. Yet we do not want you to feel overwhelmed by our ideas, adopt them unquestioningly or promote them to others in a dogmatic way because we know from experience that our own views shift on a regular basis. Therefore we see the information in this book as a starting place from which you should be free to develop your own approaches and we encourage you to question the text, discuss our ideas with colleagues/service users and develop your own embedded perspectives that relate more specifically to your local contexts.

References

Abberley, P. (1987) 'The concept of oppression and the development of a social theory of disability', *Disability, Handicap and Society*, 2 (1): 5–19.

Abberley, P. (1992) 'Counting us out: a discussion of the OPCS Disability Surveys', *Disability, Handicap and Society*, 7 (2): 139–55.

Adair, J. (1979) *Action-centred Leadership*. London: Gower.

Adams, K. (2005) *Sources of Innovation and Creativity: A Summary of the Research*. Paper commissioned by the National Center on Education and the Economy for the New Commission on the Skills of America, Washington, DC.

Adams, R., Dominelli, L. and Payne, M. (2002) *Critical Practice in Social Work*. Basingstoke: Palgrave.

Adams, S. (1996) *The Dilbert Principle*. New York and London: Harper Business.

Agar, M. (1996) *The Professional Stranger: An Informal Introduction to Ethnography*. San Diego, CA: Academic Press.

Ainscow, M. and Booth, T. (2003) *The Index for Inclusion: Developing Learning and Participation in Schools*. Bristol: Centre for Studies in Inclusive Education.

Alderson, P. (1993) *Children's Consent to Surgery*. Buckingham: Open University Press.

Alderson, P. (1995) *Listening to Children: Children, Ethics and Social Research*. Ilford: Barnardo's.

Alderson, P. (2000) *Young Children's Rights: Exploring Beliefs, Principle and Practice*. London: Jessica Kingsley.

Alderson, P. (2002) 'Student rights in British schools: trust, autonomy, connection and regulation', in R. Edwards (ed.), *Children, Home and School: Autonomy, Connection or Regulation*. London: Falmer Press.

Aldgate, J. and Tunstill, J. (1995) *Implementing Section 17 of the Children Act*. London: DoH.

Aldridge, M. and Evetts, J. (2003) 'Rethinking the concept of professionalism: the case of journalism', *British Journal of Sociology*, 54 (4): 547–64.

Alimo-Metcalfe, B., Ford, J., Harding, N. and Lawler, J. (2000) *Leadership Development in British Organisations (at the Beginning of the 21st Century)*, Careers Research Forum Report. London: Careers Research Forum.

Amabile, T. (1996) *Creativity in Context: Update to the Social Psychology of Creativity*. Boulder, CO: Westview Press.

Anning, A., Cottrell, D., Frost, N., Green, J. and Robinson, M. (2006) *Developing Multi-professional Teamwork for Integrated Children's Services*. Maidenhead: Open University Press.

Apple, M. W. and Beane, J. A. (eds) (1997). *Democratic Schools*. Alexandria, VA: Association for Supervision and Curriculum Development.

Armstrong, M. (2009) *A Handbook of Human Resource Management Practice*. London: Kogan Page.

Aubrey, C. (2010) 'Leading and working in multi-agency teams', in G. Pugh and B. Duffy (eds), *Contemporary Issues in the Early Years*. London: Sage.

Badham, B. (2000) *'So Why Don't you Get Your Own House In Order?' Towards Children and Governance in the Children's Society*. London: TCS.

Ball, J. and Sones, R. (2004) *First Nations Early Childhood Care and Development Programs as Hubs for Intersectoral Service Delivery*. Paper presented at the Second International Conference on Local and Regional Health Programmes, Quebec City, 10 October.

Ball, S. J. (2003) 'The teacher's soul and the terrors of performativity', *Journal of Education Policy*, 18 (2): 215–28.

Bank, J. (1992) *The Essence of Total Quality Management*. London: Prentice Hall.

Banks, S. (1998a) 'Codes of ethics and ethical conduct: a view from the caring professions', *Public Money and Management*, 18 (1): 27–30.

Banks, S. (1998b) 'Professional ethics in social work – what future?', *British Journal of Social Work*, 28: 213–31.

Barker, R. (ed.) (2009) *Making Sense of Every Child Matters: Multi-Professional Practice Guidance*. Bristol: Policy Press.

Barnes, C., Mercer, G. and Shakespeare, T. (1999) *Exploring Disability*. Cambridge: Polity.

Barr, H. (1996) 'Ends and means in inter-professional education: towards a typology', *Education for Health*, 9 (3): 341–52.

Bateson, G. (1973) *Steps to an Ecology of Mind*. New York: Paladin.

Bauman, Z. (1993) *Postmodern Ethics*. Oxford: Blackwell.

Beattie, A. (2007) 'Journeys into third space? Health alliances and the challenge of border crossing', in A. Leathard (ed.), *Interprofessional Collaboration: From Policy to Practice in Health and Social Care*. Hove: Brunner-Routledge.

Bell, J. (1999) *Doing Your Research Project: A Guide to First Time Researchers in Education*, 3rd edn. Oxford: Oxford University Press.

Beresford, P. (1999) *Theorising Social Work Research*, seminar on Social Work What Kinds of Knowledge, Brunel University, May.

Berg, I. K. and DeJong, P. (1996) 'Solution-building conversations: co-constructing a sense of competence with clients', *Families in Society: Journal of Contemporary Human Services*, 77: 376–91.

Bertram, T., Pascal, C., Bokhari, S., Gasper, M. and Holtermann, S. (2002) *Early Excellence Centre Pilot Programme: Second Evaluation Report 2000–2001*. Nottingham: DfES Publications.

Billingham, K. and Barnes, J. (2009) 'The role of health in early years services', in G. Pugh and B. Duffy (eds), *Contemporary Issues in the Early Years*. London: Sage.

Bilson, A. and Ross, S. (1999) *Social Work Management and Practice: Systems Principles*, 2nd edn. London: Jessica Kingsley.

Bilson, A. and Thorpe, D. H. (2007) 'Towards aesthetic seduction using emotional engagement and stories', *Kybernetes*, 36 (7/8): 936–45.

Bolden, R., Gosling, J., Marturano, A. and Dennison, P. (2003) *A Review of Leadership Theory and Competency Frameworks*. Exeter: University of Exeter, Centre for Leadership Studies.

Bolton, G. (2010) *Reflective Practice: Writing And Professional Development*. London: Sage.

Borland, M., Hill, M., Laybourn, A. and Stafford, A. (2001) *Improving Consultation with Children and Young People in Relevant Aspects of Policy-Making and Legislation in Scotland*. Edinburgh: Scottish Parliament Education, Culture and Sport Committee.

Bottery, M. (1998) *Professionals and Policy: Management Strategy in a Competitive World*. London: Cassell.

Boyne, B., Day, P. and Walker, R. (2001) 'The evaluation of public service inspection: a theoretical framework', *Urban Studies*, 39 (7): 1197–212.

Boyne, G. (2002) 'Concepts and indicators of local authority performance: an evaluation of the statutory frameworks in England and Wales', *Public Money and Management*, 22 (2): 17–24.

Boyne, G. A. (2003) 'Sources of public service improvement: a critical review and research agenda', *Journal of Public Administration Research and Theory*, 13 (4): 767–94.

Brady, A., McNicoll, L. and Davis, J. M. (2010) 'Mentoring Early Years Practitioners: Listening and Staff Development', Birmingham, 20th EECERA Annual Conference Knowledge and Voice in Early Childhood: Who Knows, Who Speaks, Who Listens?, 6-8th September 2010.

Brady, J. (2004) 'Inspecting for improvement: the knowledge imperative', article in *National Association of Independent Review Organizations News*. Sandbach, Cheshire: NAIRO.

Brech, E. (1957) *Organisation: The Framework of Management*. London: Longmans, Green.

Bricher, G. (2001) 'If You Want to Know About It Just Ask. Exploring Disabled Young People's Experiences of Health and Health Care'. Unpublished PhD, University of South Australia.

Broadhead, P., Meleady, C. and Delgado, M. A. (2008) *Children, Families and Communities: Creating and Sustaining Integrated Services*. Maidenhead: Open University Press.

Bronfenbrenner, U. (1989) 'Ecological systems theory', in R. Vasta (ed.), *Annals of Child Development*, Vol. 6. Greenwich, CT: JAI Press, pp. 187–249.

Brookfield, S. (1995) *Becoming a Critically Reflective Teacher*. San Francisco: Jossey Bass.

Brown, B. (1998) *Unlearning Discrimination in the Early Years*. Oakhill: Trentham Books.

Brown, G. (2003) 'State and market: towards a public interest test', *Political Quarterly*, 74: 266–84.

Brown, K. and White, K. (2006) *Exploring the Evidence Base for Integrated Children's Services*. Edinburgh: Scottish Executive.

Browne, N. (2004) *Gender Equity in the Early Years*. Maidenhead: Open University Press.

Bruce, A. (2009) *Beyond Barriers: Intercultural Learning and Inclusion in Globalized Paradigms*. Lisbon: EDEN.

Bruce, A. and Hartnett, T. (2005) *Community Based Learning via Learning Communities: a Joint U.S.– Irish Perspective*. Helsinki: Dipoli DKK.

Bruce, T. (2004) *Developing Learning in Early Childhood*. London: Sage.

Bruner, C. (2006) 'Developing an outcome evaluation framework for use by family support programs', in P. Dolan, J. Canavan and J. Pinkerton (eds), *Family Support as Reflective Practice*. London: Jessica Kingsley, pp. 237–49.

Bruner, J. (1996) *The Culture of Education*. Cambridge, MA: Harvard University Press.

Buchanan, D., Claydon, T. and Doyle, M. (1999) 'Organisational development and change: the legacy of the nineties', *Human Resource Management Journal*, 9 (2): 20–36.

Burns, J. M. (1978) *Leadership*. New York: Harper & Row.

Burns, T. and Stalker, G. M. (1961) *The Management of Innovation*. London: Tavistock.

Cairns, L. (2001) 'Investing In Children: learning how to promote the rights of all children', *Children and Society*, 15 (5): 347–60.

Cairns, L. (2006) 'Participation with purpose', in K. Tisdall, J. Davis, M. Hill and A. Prout (eds), *Children, Childhood and Social Inclusion*. London: Policy Press.

Cameron, C. (2006) *New Ways of Educating: Pedagogy and Children's Services*. London: Thomas Coram Research Unit, Institute of Education, University of London.

Cameron, K. and Freeman, J. (1991) 'Cultural congruence, strength and type: relationships to effectiveness', *Research in Organizational Change and Development*, 5: 23–58.

Campbell, J. and Oliver, M. (1996) *Disability Politics: Understanding Our Past, Changing Our Future*. London: Routledge.

Carlyle, T. (1869) *On Heroes, Hero-Worship, and the Heroic in History*. London: Chapman & Hall.

Carneiro, R. (2007) 'The big picture: understanding learning and meta-learning challenges', *European Journal of Education*, 42 (2): 151–72.

Carpenter, B. (1997) *Families in Context: Emerging Trends in Family Support and Early Intervention*. London: Fulton.

Carpenter, J. and Dickinson, H. (2008) *Inter-professional Education and Training*. Bristol: Policy Press.

Carr, D. (1999) 'Professional education and professional ethics', *Journal of Applied Philosophy*, 16 (1): 190–9.

Carr-Saunders, A. M. (1955) 'Metropolitan conditions and traditional professional relationships', in R. M. Fischer (ed.), *The Metropolis in Modern Life*. New York: Doubleday.

Cattell, R. B. (1963) *The Sixteen Personality Factor Questionnaire*. Champaign, IL: Institute for Personality and Ability Training.

CEDEFOP (2008) *Terminology of European Education and Training Policy: A Selection of 100 Key Terms*. Luxembourg: Office for Official Publications of the European Communities.

Chan Kim, W. and and Mauborge, R. (2005) *Blue Ocean Strategy: How to Create Uncontested Market Space and Make Competition Irrelevant*. Cambridge, MA: Harvard Business School Press.

Chaskin, R. J. (2006) 'Family support as community-based practice: considering a community capacity framework for family support provision', in P. Dolan, J. Canavan and J. Pinkerton (eds), *Family Support as Reflective Practice*. London: Jessica Kingsley.

Chawala, L. (2001) 'Evaluating children's participation: seeking areas of consensus', *Participatory Learning and Action Notes*, 42: 9–13.

Checkland, P. and Scholes, J. (1990) *Soft Systems Methodology in Action*. Chichester: John Wiley.

Children in Scotland (2008) *Working It Out: Developing the Children's Sector Workforce*. Edinburgh: Children in Scotland.

Children's Society, The (2000) *The Children and Young People's Participation Initiative*. London: TCS.

Chomsky, N. (1977) *Essays on Form and Interpretation*. Amsterdam: North Holland.

Chomsky, N. (1988) *Language and Problems of Knowledge*. Cambridge, MA: MIT Press.

Chomsky, N. (2000) *On Nature and Language*. New York: Cambridge University Press.

Christie, D. and Menmuir, J. (2005) 'Supporting interprofessional collaboration in Scotland through a common standards framework', *Policy Futures in Education*, 3 (1): 62–74.

Clarke, J. (2008) 'Performance paradoxes: the politics of evaluation in public services', in H. Davis and S. Martin (eds), *Public Services Inspection in the UK*, Research Highlights in Social Work 50. London: Jessica Kingsley.

Clutterbuck, D. (2008) 'What is happening in coaching and mentoring? And what is the difference between them?', *Development in Learning Organizations*, 22 (4): 8–10.

Coalition of Childhood Umbrella Organisations (CCUO) (2011) *Guidance for Mentoring in Childhood Practice*. Dundee: Scottish Social Services Council.

Cockburn, T. (1998) 'Children and citizenship in Britain', *Childhood*, 5 (1): 99–118.

Cockburn, T. (2002) *Concepts of Social Inclusion/Exclusion and Childhoods*. Paper presented at ESRC Children and Social Inclusion Seminar, University of Edinburgh, December.

Cockburn, T. (2010) 'Children and deliberative democracy', in B. Percy-Smith and N. Thomas (eds), *A Handbook of Children and Young People's Participation*. Abingdon: Routledge.

Cohen, B., Moss, P., Petrie, P. and Wallace, J. (2004) *A New Deal for Children? Re-Forming Education and Care in England, Scotland and Sweden*. Bristol: Policy Press.

Collins, J. (2008) Developing positive relationships', in P. Foley and S. Leverett (eds), *Connecting with Children: Developing Positive Relationships*. Bristol: Policy Press.

Collins, R. (1990) 'Changing conceptions in the sociology of the professions', in R. Torstendahl and M. Burrage (eds), *The Formation of Professions: Knowledge, State and Strategy*. London: Sage, pp. 11–23.

Cooper, J. E. (2002) 'Constructivist leadership: its evolving narrative', in L. Lambert, D. Walker, D. P. Zimmermann, J. E. Cooper, M. Dale, M. D. Lambert, M. E. Gardner and M. Szabo (eds), *The Constructivist Leader*, 2nd edn. Oxford, OH: Teachers College Press.

Corker, M. and Davis, J. M. (2000) 'Disabled children – invisible under the law', in J. Cooper and S. Vernon (eds), *Disability and the Law*. London: Jessica Kingsley.

Corker, M. and Davis, J. M. (2001) 'Portrait of Callum: the disabling of a childhood', in R. Edwards (ed.), *Children, Home and School: Autonomy, Connection or Regulation*. London: Falmer Press.

Corker, M. and Shakespeare, T. (2001) 'Mapping the terrain', in M. Corker and T. Shakespeare (eds), *Disability and Postmodernity*. London: Continuum.

Coulshed, V., Mullender, A., Jones, D. N. and Thompson, N. (2006) *Management in Social Work*, 3rd edn. Basingstoke: Palgrave Macmillan.

Cowan, R. (1996) 'Perfomativity, post-modernity and the university', *Comparative Education*, 32 (2): 245–58.

Cropley, A. J. and Cropley D. H. (2009) *Fostering Creativity: A Diagnostic Approach for Higher Education and Organisations*. Cresskill, NJ: Hampton Press.

Csikszentmihalyi, M. (1996) *Creativity: Flow and the Psychology of Discovery and Invention*. New York: Harper Perennial/Harvard Business School Press.

Cummins, J. (2000) *Language, Power and Pedagogy: Bilingual Children in the Crossfire*. Clevedon: Multilingual Matters.

Cutler, D. and Taylor, A. (2003) *Expanding Involvement: A Snapshot of Participation Infrastructure for Young People Living in England*. Carnegie UK Trust/Department for Education and Skills.

Dahlberg, G., Moss, P. and Pence, A. (1999) *Beyond Quality in Early Childhood Education and Care: Postmodern Perspectives*. London: Falmer Press.

Dahlberg, G., Moss, P. and Pence, A. (2007) *Beyond Quality in Early Childhood Education and Care: Languages of Evaluation*, 2nd edn. London: Falmer Press.

Daniel, B. and Wassell, S. (2002) *Assessing and Promoting Resilience in Vulnerable Children*. London: Jessica Kingsley.

David, T., Powell, S. and Goouch, K. (2010) 'The world picture', in G. Pugh and B. Duffy (eds) *Contemporary Issues in the Early Years*. London: Sage.

Davis, J. M. (1996) *Sport for All?* PhD thesis, University of Edinburgh.

Davis, J. M. (1998) 'Understanding the meanings of children: a reflexive process', *Children and Society*, 12 (3): 25–33.

Davis, J. M. (2001) *After School Clubs Provision for Children With 'Special*

Needs'. Report for Midlothian Association of Play and Midlothian Childcare and Early Years Partnership.

Davis, J. M. (2006) 'Disability, childhood studies and the construction of medical discourses: questioning attention deficit hyperactivity disorder – a theoretical perspective', in G. Lloyd, J. Stead and D. Cohen (eds), *Critical New Perspectives on ADHD*. London: Taylor & Francis.

Davis, J. M. (2007) 'Analysing participation and social exclusion with children and young people: lessons from practice', *International Journal of Children's Rights*, 15 (1): 121–46.

Davis, J. M. (2009) 'Involving children', in K. Tisdall, J. Davis and M. Gallagher (eds), *Researching with Children and Young People: Research Design, Methods and Analysis*. London: Sage.

Davis, J. M. (2011) *Integrated Children's Services*. London: Sage.

Davis, J. M. and Edwards, R. (eds) (2004) 'Setting the agenda: social inclusion, children and young people', *Children and Society*, 18(2): 97–105.

Davis, J. M. and Hogan, J. (2004) 'Research with children: ethnography, participation, disability, self-empowerment', in C. Barnes and G. Mercer (eds), *Implementing the Social Model of Disability: Theory and Research*. Leeds: Disability Press.

Davis, J. M. and Hughes, A. with Kilgore, J., Whiting, C. and Abbott, J. (2005) *Early Years Workforce Competencies Review* Edinburgh: City of Edinburgh Council/University of Edinburgh.

Davis, J. M. and Watson, N. (2000) 'Disabled children's rights in everyday life: problematising notions of competency and promoting self-empowerment', *International Journal of Children's Rights*, 8: 211–28.

Davis, J. M. and Watson, N. (2001) 'Where are the children's experiences? Analysing social and cultural exclusion in "special" and "mainstream" schools', *Disability and Society*, 16 (5): 671–87.

Davis, J. M. and Watson, N. (2002) 'Countering stereotypes of disability: disabled children and resistance', in M. Corker and T. Shakespeare (eds), *Disability and Postmodernity*. London: Continuum.

Davis, J. M. et al. (2011) *Embedding Vision: Final Report of the CREANOVA Project*. Edinburgh: Edinburgh University Press. A project funded by the Education, Audiovisual and Culture Executive Agency (EACEA) of the European Commission, Project No. 143725-LLP-1-2008-1-ES-KA1-KA1SCR.

De Shazer, S. and Molnar, A. (1987) 'Solution-focused therapy: toward the identification of therapeutic tasks', *Journal of Marital and Family Therapy*, 13 (4): 349–58.

Deming, W. E. (1982) *Out of Crisis*. London: Gurteen Knowledge.

Department for Education (DfE) (2011) *Foreword: Children and Young People Strategy.* London: DfE.

Department for Education and Skills (DfES) (2003) *Every Child Matters.* Norwich: The Stationery Office.

Department for Education and Skills (DfES) (2004a) *Every Child Matters: The Next Steps.* Nottingham: DfES Publications.

Department for Education and Skills (DfES) (2004b) *Effective Provision of Pre-School Education (EPPE) Study.* London: DfES.

Department of Health (DoH) (2003) *Child Protection: Messages from Research.* London: DoH.

Derman-Sparks, L. (1989) *Anti-bias Curriculum: Tools for Empowering Young Children.* Washington, DC: National Association for the Education of Young Children.

Dewey, J. (1938) *Experience and Education.* New York: Collier Books.

Dickson, G. (1995) 'Principles of risk management', *Quality in Health Care,* 4 (2): 75–9.

Dilthey, W. (1900) 'The development of hermeneutics', in H. P. Rickman (ed.), *W. Dilthey Selected Writings.* Cambridge: Cambridge University Press.

Dodgson, M. (1993) 'Organizational learning: a review of some literatures', *Organization Studies,* 14 (3): 375–94.

Dolan, P. (2006a) 'Family support: from description to reflection', in P. Dolan, J. Canavan and J. Pinkerton (eds), *Family Support as Reflective Practice.* London: Jessica Kingsley.

Dolan, P. (2006b) 'Assessment, intervention and self-appraisal tools for family support', in P. Dolan, J. Canavan and J. Pinkerton (eds), *Family Support as Reflective Practice.* London: Jessica Kingsley.

Dolan, P. (2008) 'Social support, social justice and social capital: a tentative theoretical triad for community development', *Community Development,* 39 (1): 112–19.

Dolan, P. and McGrath, B. (2006) 'Enhancing support for young people in need: reflections on informal and formal sources of help', in P. Dolan, J. Canavan and H. Pinkerton (eds), *Family Support as Reflective Practice.* London: Jessica Kingsley.

Dolan, P., Canavan, J. and Pinkerton, J. (eds) (2006) *Family Support as Reflective Practice.* London: Jessica Kingsley.

Dorrian, A.-M., Tisdall, K. and Hamilton, D. (2001) *Taking the Initiative: Promoting Young People's Participation in Public Decision Making in Scotland.* London: Carnegie Young People Initiative.

Drucker, P. (2007) *The Effective Executive: The Definitive Guide to Getting the Right Things Done.* Oxford: Butterworth-Heinemann.

Drucker, P. F. (1974) *Management: Tasks, Responsibilities, Practices.* New York: Harper & Row.

Drummond, H. (1993) *The Quality Movement.* London: Kogan Page.

Dundee Council (2009) *Report to the Dundee Child Protection Committee into the Death of Brandon Muir.* Dundee: Dundee Council.

Edwards, R. and Nicoll, K. (2006) 'Expertise, competence and reflection in the rhetoric of professional development', *British Educational Research Journal*, 32 (1): 115–31.

Engeström, Y. (2004) 'Managing as argumentative history-making', in R. Boland (ed.), *Managing as Designing.* Stanford, CA: Stanford University Press.

Engeström, Y. and Escalante, V. (1995) 'Mundane tool or object of affection? The rise and fall of the postal buddy', in B. Nardi (ed.), *Activity Theory and Human-Computer Interaction.* Cambridge, MA: MIT Press, pp. 325–73.

Etzioni, A. (1964) *Modern Organizations.* Englewood Cliffs, NJ: Prentice Hall.

Etzioni, A. (1993) *The Spirit of Community: Rights, Responsibility, and the Communitarian Agenda.* New York: Crown.

European Commission (2006) *Implementing the Community Lisbon Programme. Proposal for a Recommendation of the European Parliament and of the Council on the Establishment of the European Qualifications Framework for Lifelong Learning.* Luxembourg: Office for Official Publications of the European Communities.

European Foundation for Quality Management (EFQM) (2011) *Introducing the Excellence Model.* Brussels: EFQM.

Evans, J. and Lunt, I. (2002) 'Inclusive education: are there limits?', *European Journal of 'Special Needs' Education*, 17 (1): 1–14.

Fagerberg, J. (2003) *Innovation: A Guide to the Literature.* Oslo: Centre for Technology, Innovation and Culture, University of Oslo.

Farnham, D. and Horton, S. (eds) (1996) *Managing the New Public Services.* Basingstoke. Macmillan.

Farrier, S., Quinn, K., Bruce, A., Davis, J. M. and Bizas, N. (2011) *Supporting ICT Situated Learning and Virtual Skills Rehearsal in Workforce Development.* Paper presented at the European Distance and E-Learning Network (EDEN) annual conference, June, Dublin.

Fayol, H. (1949) *General and Industrial Management*, translated from the French edition (Dunod) by Constance Storrs. London: Pitman.

Fergusson, R. (2000) 'Modernizing managerialism in education', in J. Clarke, S. Gewirtz and E. McLaughlin (eds), *New Managerialism, New Welfare.* London: Sage.

Ferrar, P. (2004) 'Reflections from the field: defying definition: competences in coaching and mentoring', *International Journal of Evidence-Based Coaching and Mentoring*, 2 (2): 53–60.

Figuerdo, A. (2009) *Innovating in Education: Educating for Innovation.* Porto: EDEN Research Workshop.

Finer, C. J. and Hundt, G. L. (2000) 'The business of research: issues of politics and practice', Editorial Introduction, *Social Policy and Administration*, 34 (4): 361–4.

Finkelstein, V. (1993) 'The commonality of disability', in J. Swain, V. Finkelstein, S. French and M. Oliver (eds), *Disabling Barriers: Enabling Environments*. London: Sage in association with the Open University.

Fitzgerald, D. and Kay, J. (2008) *Working Together in Children's Services*. Abingdon: Routledge.

Fitzgerald, R., Graham, A., Smith, A. and Taylor, N. (2010) 'Children's participation as a struggle over recognition: exploring the promise of dialogue', in B. Percy-Smith and N. Thomas (eds), *A Handbook of Children and Young People's Participation*. Abingdon: Routledge.

Fletcher, J. (2004) 'Invisible work: the disappearing of relational practice at work', in Ohio State University President's Council on Women's Issues, *Annual Report*. Ohio: Ohio State University, pp. 28–33.

Flynn, N. (1990) *Public Sector Management*. London: Harvester Wheatsheaf.

Foley, P. (2008) 'Reflecting on skills for work with children', in P. Foley and A. Rixon (eds), *Changing Children's Services: Working and Learning Together*. Bristol: Policy Press.

Foley, P. and Rixon, A. (2008) *Changing Children's Services: Working and Learning Together*. Bristol: Policy Press

Ford, J. and Lawler, J. (2007) 'Blending existentialist and constructionist approaches in leadership studies: an exploratory account', *Leadership and Organization Development Journal*, 28 (5): 409–25.

Fox, A. (2005) 'Bringing it together: the role of the programme manager', in J. Weinberger, C. Pickstone and P. Hannon (eds), *Learning from Sure Start: Working with Young Children and Their Families*. Maidenhead: Open University Press.

Francis, M. and Lorenzo, R. (2002) 'Seven realms of children's participation', *Journal of Environmental Psychology*, 22: 157–16.

Fraser, N. (1997) *Justice Interruptus*. London: Routledge.

Freeman, T. (2002) 'Using performance indicators to improve health care quality in the public sector: a review of the literature', *Health Services Management Research*, 15: 126–37.

Freidson, E. (1994) *Professionalism Reborn: Theory, Prophecy and Policy*. Cambridge: Polity.

Freire, P. (1970) *Pedagogy of the Oppressed*. London: Penguin Press.

Freire, P. (1997) *Pedagogy of the Heart*. New York: Continuum Press.

French, J. P. and Raven, B. H. (1986) 'The bases of social power', in D. Cartwright and A. F. Zander (eds), *Group Dynamics: Research and Theory*, 3rd edn. New York: Harper & Row.

Friedman, M. (2000) *Reforming Financing for Family and Children's Services*. Sacramento: CA: Foundation Consortium.

Friedson, E. (1983) 'The theory of professions: state of the art', in R. Dingwall and P. Lewis (eds), *The Sociology of the Professions*. London and Basingstoke: Macmillan.

Frost, N. (2001) 'Professionalism, change and the politics of lifelong learning', *Studies In Continuing Education*, 23 (1): 5–17.

Frost, N. (2005) 'A problematic relationship? Evidence and practice in the workplace', in A. Bilson (ed.), *Evidence-Based Practice in Social Work*. London: Whitting & Birch.

Frost, N., Robinson, M. and Anning, A. (2005) 'Social workers in multidisciplinary teams: issues and dilemmas for professional practice', *Child and Family Social Work*, 10: 187–96.

Gabriel, J. (1998) *A Preliminary Analysis of Children and Young People's Participation in The Children's Society*. London: TCS.

Gardener, R. (2006) 'Safeguarding children through supporting families', in P. Dolan, J. Canavan and J. Pinkerton (eds), *Family Support as Reflective Practice*. London: Jessica Kingsley.

Garvey, B. and Galloway, K. (2002) 'Mentoring at Halifax plc (HBOS) – a small beginning in a large organisation', *Career Development International*. Online at: http://www.emeraldinsight.com/1362-0436.htm.

Garvey, R., Stokes, P. and Megginson, D. (2009) *Coaching and Mentoring: Theory and Practice*. London: Sage.

Gasper, M. (2010) *Multi-Agency Working in the Early Years: Challenges and Opportunities*. London: Sage.

Gewirtz, S. (2006) 'Towards a contextualised analysis of social justice in education', *Educational Philosophy and Theory*, 38 (1): 69–81.

Giddens, A. (2004) *The Third Way: The Renewal of Social Democracy*. Oxford: Polity Press.

Gilbert, J. and Bainbridge, L. (2003) 'Canada – interprofessional education and collaboration: theoretical challenges, practical solutions', in A. Leathard (ed.), *Interprofessional Collaboration: From Policy to Practice in Health and Social Care*. Hove: Brunner-Routledge.

Gilligan, R. (2000) 'Family support: issues and prospects', in J. Canavan, P. Dolan and J. Pinkerton (eds), *Family Support: Diversion from Diversity*. London: Jessica Kingsley.

Glennie, S. (2007) 'Safeguarding children together: addressing the interprofessional agenda', in A. Leathard (ed.), *Interprofessional Collaboration: From Policy to Practice in Health and Social Care*. Abingdon: Routledge.

Glenny, G. and Roaf, C. (2008) *Multiprofessional Communication: Making Systems Work for Children*. Maidenhead: Open University Press and McGraw-Hill Education.

Goleman, D. (1996) *Emotional Intelligence*. London: Bloomsbury.

Goodlad, J. L. (1997) *In Praise of Education*. New York: Teachers College Press.

Graham, P. and Machin, A. I. (2009) 'Interprofessional working and the children's workforce', in R. Barker (ed.), *Making Sense of Every Child Matters*. Bristol: Policy Press.

Griffiths, M. (2003) *Action for Social Justice in Education: Fairly Different*. Buckingham: Open University Press.

Grint, K. (2005) *Leadership: Limits and Possibilities*. Basingstoke: Palgrave Macmillan.

Grossek, H. (2008) *To What Extent Does Coaching Contribute to the Professional Development of Teachers?* Research Project Report, Education and Policy Research Division, Department of Education and Early Childhood Development.

Gulick, L. and Urwick, L. (eds) (1937) *Papers on the Science of Administration*. New York: Institute of Public Administration.

H.M. Treasury (2003) *Every Child Matters Report*. Presented to Parliament, September.

Habermas, J. (1984) *Reason and the Rationalization of Society*, Vol. 1 of *The Theory of Communicative Action*, trans. Thomas McCarthy. Boston: Beacon Press.

Habermas, J. (1987) *The Theory of Communicative Action*, Vol. 2, *System and Lifeworld: A Critique of Functionalist Reason*. Boston: Beacon Press.

Hafford-Letchfield, T. (2006) *Management and Organisations in Social Work*. Exeter: Learning Matters.

Halmos, P. (1973) *Professionalisation and Social Change*, Sociological Review Monographs, 20, p. 11.

Halone, K. and Pecchioni, L. (2001) 'Relational listening: a grounded theoretical model', *Communication Reports*, 14 (2): 59–71.

Hämäläinen, T. J. (2005) *Structural Adjustment and Social Innovations: The New Challenge for Innovation Policies*. Online at: http://www.sitra.fi.

Hämäläinen, T. J. and Heiskala, R. (2007) *Social Innovations, Institutional Change and Economic Performance: Making Sense of Structural Adjustment Processes in Industrial Sectors, Regions and Societies*. Cheltenham: Edward Elgar.

Hammer, M. and Champy, J. A. (1993) *Reengineering the Corporation: A Manifesto for Business Revolution*. New York: Harper Business Books.

Hannon, P., Weinberger, J., Pickstone, C. and Fox, A. (2005) 'Looking to the future', in J. Weinberger, C. Pickstone and P. Hannon (eds), *Learning from Sure Start: Working with Young Children and Their Families*. Maidenhead: Open University Press.

Hargie, O. and Dickson, D. (2006) *Skilled Interpersonal Communication*. Abingdon: Routledge.

Hargreaves, A. (2003) *Teaching in the Knowledge Society: Education in the Age of Insecurity*. Maidenhead: Open University Press.

Harker, R. M., Dobel-Ober, D., Berridge, D. and Sinclair, R. (2004) 'More than the sum of its parts? Inter-professional working in the education of looked after children', *Children and Society*, 18 (3): 179–93.

Harris, J. (2003) *The Social Work Business*. London: Routledge.

Harrison, S. (1999) *New Labour, Modernisation and Health Care Governance*. Paper presented at the Political Studies Association/Social Policy Association Conference New Labour, New Health, London, September.

Harrison, S. (2002) 'New Labour, modernisation and the medical labour process', *Journal of Social Policy*, 31 (3): 465–85.

Hart, R. J. (1992) *Children's Participation: From Tokenism to Citizenship*. Florence: UNICEF/Save the Children.

Hatcher, R. and LeBlond, D. (2001) 'Education Action Zones and Zones d'Education Prioritaires', in S. Riddell and L. Tett (eds), *Education, Social Justice and Inter-Agency Working: Joined Up or Fractured Policy?* London: Routledge.

Haug, M. R. (1973) *Deprofessionalization: An Alternative Hypothesis for the Future*, Sociological Review Monographs, 20, pp. 195–211.

Healy, K. and Meagher, G. (2004) 'The reprofessionalization of social work: collaborative approaches for achieving professional recognition', *British Journal of Social Work*, 34: 243–60.

Hezlett, S. A. (2005) 'Protégés' learning and mentoring relationships: a review of the literature and exploratory case study', *Advances in Developing Human Resources*, 7 (4): 505–26.

Hill, C. and Jones, G. (1995) *Strategic Management: An Integrated Approach*, 3rd edn. Boston: Houghton Mifflin.

Hill, M. (1997) *The Policy Process in the Modern State*, 3rd edn. Herts: Prentice Hall.

Hill, M. and Tisdall, K. (1997) *Children and Society*. Harlow: Longman.

Hill, M., Davis, J., Prout, A. and Tisdall K. (eds) (2004) 'Children, young people and participation', *Children and Society*, 18 (2): 77–176.

Hogan, J. (2003) *Rhetoric or Reality*. MA thesis, University of Liverpool.

Holy, L. (1984) 'Theory methodology and the research process', in R. Ellen (ed.), *Ethnographic Research*. London: Academic Press.

Honneth, A. (2000) *Suffering from Indeterminacy: An Attempt at a Reactualisation of Hegel's Philosophy of Right, Two Lectures*. Assen: Van Gorcum.

Hough, M. (2010) *Counselling Skills and Theory*, 3rd edn. Oxford: Hodder Education.

Hughes, A. and Davis, J. (2005) *Workforce Competences in Early Education, Childcare and Playwork: A Review of the Literature*. Edinburgh.

Huxham, C. and Macdonald, D. (1992) 'Introducing collaborative advantage: achieving inter-organisational effectiveness through meta-strategy', *Management Decision*, 30 (3): 50–6.

Hyland, S. (1997) *Will Adults Really Let Us?* Manchester: TCS/ Manchester University.

Ibáñez, J., Fernández, I., Arandia, M., Eizagirre, A., Barandiaran, M., Etxebarria, I. et al. (2010) *Discovering Vision: Theoretical Foundations and Practical Solutions in the Field of Creative Learning.* Report from the Creative Learning and Networking for European Innovation, a project funded by the Education, Audiovisual and Culture Executive Agency (EACEA) of the European Commission, Project No. 143725-LLP-1-2008-1-ES-KA1-KA1SCR.

Ingram, A. (2008) *Working It Out: Developing the Children's Sector Workforce.* Edinburgh: Children in Scotland.

ISO (2004) *Guidance on the Concept and Use of the Process Approach for Management Systems.* London: BSI Standards.

Jack, G. (1997) 'An ecological approach to social work with children and families', *Child and Family Social Work*, 2 (2): 109–20.

Jack, G. (2006) 'The area and community components of children's well-being', *Children and Society*, 20 (5): 334–47.

Jackson, M. C. (1991) 'Five commitments of critical systems theory', in R. B. Blackham, R. L. Flood and M. C. Jackson (eds), *Systems Thinking in Europe.* London: Plenum Press.

James, A. and Prout, A. (1990) 'Contemporary issues in the sociological study of childhood', in A. James and A. Prout (eds), *Constructing and Reconstructing Childhood.* London: Falmer.

Jaussi, M. L. (2002) *Euskadi Learning Communities.* Vitoria: Publications of the Basque Government.

Jaussi, M. L. (2002) *Learning Communities in Euskadi.* Vitoria: Department of Education, Universities and Research of the Basque Government.

Jeffree, C. and Fox, G. (1998) 'Managing self and others', in J. Taylor and M. Woods (eds), *Early Childhood Studies – Managing Holistic Introduction.* Bath: Bath Press.

Jeffrey, L. (2003) 'Moving on from child protection: messages from research and re-focusing', in N. Frost, A. Lloyd and L. Jeffrey, L. (eds), *The RHP Companion To Family Support.* Lyme Regis: Russell House.

Johnson, T. J. (1972) *Professions and Power.* London: Macmillan.

Jones, C. and Jowett, V. (1997) *Managing Facilities.* Butterworth-Heinemann.

Jones. C and Leverett, S. (2008) 'Policy into practice: assessment, evaluation and multi-agency working with children', in P. Foley and A. Rixon (eds), *Changing Children's Services: Working and Learning Together*. Bristol: Policy Press.

Kanter, R. M. (1988) 'When a thousand flowers bloom: structural, collective, and social conditions for innovation in organizations', in B. M. Staw and L. L. Cummings (eds), *Research in Organizational Behavior*. Greenwich, CT: JAI Press.

Kaplan, R. and Norton, D. (1992) 'The balanced scorecard: measures that drive performance', *Harvard Business Review*, January/February, pp. 71–9.

Katz, D. and Kahn, R. (1966) *The Social Psychology of Organisations*. New York: John Wiley.

Kelley, H. H. (1967) 'Attribution theory in social psychology', in D. Levine (ed.), *Nebraska Symposium on Motivation*. Lincoln, NB: University of Nebraska Press.

Kirby, P. with Bryson, S. (2002) *Measuring the Magic? Evaluating Young People's Participation in Public Decision-Making*. London: Carnegie Young People Initiative.

Kirby, P., Lanyon, C., Cronin, K. and Sinclair, R. (2003) *Building a Culture of Participation: Involving Young People in Policy, Service Planning, Delivery and Evaluation*, Research Report. London: Department for Education and Skills.

Kolb, D. (1984) *Experiential Learning: Experience as the Source of Learning and Development*. Englewood Cliffs, NJ: Prentice Hall.

Konstantoni, K. (2011) *Young Children's Perceptions and Constructions of Social Identities and Social Implications: Promoting Social Justice in Early Childhood*. Edinburgh: Edinburgh University Press.

Laird, D. (1985) *Approaches to Training and Development*. Reading, MA: Addison-Wesley.

Land, F. F. (2000) 'Evaluation in a socio-technical context', in R. Basskerville, J. Stage and J. I. DeGross (eds), *Organizational and Social Perspectives on Information Technology*. Boston: Kluwer Academic, pp. 115–26.

Langan, M. (1993) 'New mixed economy of welfare', in J. A. Clarke (ed.), *Crisis in Care: Challenges to Social Work*. London: Sage.

Lansdown, G. (2001) *Promoting Children's Participation in Democratic Decision Making*. Florence: UNICEF.

Larson, M. S. (1997) *The Rise of Professionalism*. Berkeley, CA: University of California Press.

Lawler, J. and Bilson, A. (2010) *Social Work Management and Leadership: Managing Complexity with Creativity*. Abingdon: Routledge.

Leathard, A. (ed.) (1997) *Going Interprofessional: Working Together for Health and Welfare*. London: Routledge.

Leathard, A. (2003a) 'Models for interprofessional collaboration', in A.

Leathard (ed.), *Interprofessional Collaboration: From Policy to Practice in Health and Social Care*. Hove: Brunner-Routledge.

Leathard, A. (2003b) 'Introduction', in A. Leathard (ed.), *Interprofessional Collaboration: From Policy to Practice in Health and Social Care*. Hove: Brunner-Routledge.

Leathard, A. (ed.) (2007) *Interprofessional Collaboration: From Policy to Practice in Health and Social Care*. Hove: Brunner-Routledge.

Legge, K. (2005) *Human Resource Management: Rhetorics and Realities*. Basingstoke: Macmillan.

Léveillé, S. and Chamberland, C. (2010) 'Toward a general model for child welfare and protection services: a meta-evaluation of international experiences regarding the adoption of the Framework for the Assessment of Children in Need and Their Families (FACNF)', *Children and Youth Services Review*, 32 (7): 929–44.

Leverett, S. (2008) *Working with Young People*. London: Sage.

Levitas, R. (2005) *The Inclusive Society? Social Exclusion and New Labour*, 2nd edn. Basingstoke: Palgrave Macmillan.

Ling, T. (2000) 'Unpacking partnership: the case of health care', in J. Clarke, S. Gewirtz and E. McLaughlin (eds), *New Managerialism: New Welfare*. London: Sage.

Little, M. (1999) 'Prevention and early intervention with children in need: definition, principles and examples of good practice', *Children and Society*, 12: 304–16.

Lloyd, G., Stead, J. and Kendrick, A. (2001) *Hang On In There: A Study of Inter-Agency Work to Prevent School Exclusion in Three Local Authorities*. London: National Children's Bureau.

Locke, E. A. (1982) 'The ideas of Frederick Taylor', *Academy of Management Review*, 7 (1): 14–24.

Locock, L. (2001) *Maps and Journeys: Redesign in the NHS*. Birmingham: University of Birmingham Health Services Management Centre.

Lyus, V. (1998) *Effective Leadership and Management in the Early Years*. London: Hodder & Stoughton.

McClelland, D. C. (1961) *The Achieving Society*. Princeton, NJ: Van Nostrand.

McCoy, T. J. (1992) *Compensation and Motivation: Maximizing Employee Performance with Behavior-Based Incentive Plans*. New York: AMACOM, a division of American Management Association.

MacDonald, K. (1995) *The Sociology of the Professions*. London: Sage.

McGhee, J. and Waterhouse, L. (2002) 'Family support and the Scottish hearing system', *Child and Family Social Work*, 7: 273–83.

McGregor, D. (1960) *The Human Side of Enterprise*. New York: McGraw-Hill.

McIver, S. (2002) *Review of Public Administration in Northern Ireland*, Briefing Paper: Quality of Service, Office of the First Minister/ Deputy First Minister, Northern Ireland.

McKenzie, J. (2010) *Family Learning: Engaging with Parents*. Edinburgh: Dunedin.

McKimm, J., Jollie, C. and Hatter, M. (2007) *Mentoring Theory and Practice* (developed from the Preparedness to Practice Mentoring Scheme). London: Imperial College of Medicine.

MacNaughton, G. (2000) *Rethinking Gender In Early Childhood Education*. London: Paul Chapman.

McNicoll, L., Davis, J. M. with Aruldoss, V. (2010) *Advanced Mentoring in Childhood Practice: Course Evaluation Report*. Edinburgh: University of Edinburgh.

Maitney, P. (1997) *Practising Participation – Children in Society and the Children's Society Practitioners*. Milton Keynes: Open University Press.

Malin, N. and Morrow, G. (2007) 'Models of interprofessional working within a Sure Start "Trailblazer" Programme', *Journal of Interprofessional Care*, 21 (4): 445–57.

Malone, K. and Hartung, C. (2010) 'Challenges of participatory practice with children', in B. Percy-Smith and N. Thomas (eds), *A Handbook of Children and Young People's Participation*. Abingdon: Routledge.

Marks, E. (1994) *Case Management in Service Integration: A Concept Paper*. New York: National Centre for Children in Poverty, Columbia University School of Public Health.

Maslow, A. (1954) *Motivation and Personality*. New York: Harper.

Maturana, H. R. and Bunnell, P. (1998) *Biosphere, Homosphere, and Robosphere: What Has That to Do with Business?* Cambridge, MA: Society for Organizational Learning.

Mayall, B. (1994) *Negotiating Health: Primary School Children at Home and School*. London: Cassell.

Mayall, B. (1996) *Children Health and the Social Order*. Buckingham: Open University Press.

Mayall, B. (1998) 'Towards a sociology of child health', *Sociology of Health and Illness*, 20: 269–88.

Mayall, B. (2000) 'Conversations with children: working with generational issues', in P. Christensen and A. James (eds), *Research with Children*. London: Falmer.

Mayo, E. (1945) *The Social Problems of an Industrial Civilization*. Cambridge, MA: Harvard Business School Press.

Mazutis, D. and Slawinski, N. (2008) 'Leading organizational learning through authentic dialogue', *Management Learning*, 39: 437–56.

Megginson, D. and Clutterbuck, D. (1995) *Mentoring in Action: A Practical Guide for Managers*. Oxford: Butterworth-Heinemann.

Megginson, D. and Clutterbuck, D. (2009) *Techniques for Coaching and Mentoring*. Oxford: Butterworth-Heinemann.

Millar, M. (2006) 'A comparative perspective: exploring the space of family support', in P. Dolan, J. Canavan and J. Pinkerton (eds), *Family Support as Reflective Practice*. London: Jessica Kingsley.

Miller, E. J. and Rice, A. K. (1967) *Systems of Organization*. London: Tavistock.

Miller, G. and De Shazer, S. (2000) 'Emotions in solution-focused therapy: a re-examination', *Family Process*, 39: 5–23.

Miller, R. (2003) *Future of Tertiary Education*. Paris: OECD/CERI.

Milne, V. (2005) *Joined Up Working in the Scottish Executive*, Research Findings No. 17. Edinburgh: Office of Chief Researcher, Scottish Executive.

Mingers, J. (1992) 'Recent developments in critical management science', *Journal of the Operational Research Society*, 43 (1): 1–10.

Mintzberg, H. (1987) 'Crafting strategy', *Harvard Business Review*, 87 (4): 66–75.

Mitleton-Kelly, E. (2003) *Complex Systems and Evolutionary Perspectives on Organizations: The Application of Complexity Theory to Organizations*. Oxford: Pergamon.

Moore, S., Tulk, W. and Mitchell, R. (2005) 'Qallunaat Crossing: the Southern–Northern divide and promising practices for Canada's Inuit young people', *First Peoples Child and Family Review*, 2 (1): 117–29.

Morgan, C. and Murgatroyd, S. (1994) *Total Quality Management in the Public Sector: An International Perspective*. Buckingham: Open University Press.

Morgan, G. (1986) *Images of Organization*. Thousand Oaks, CA and London: Sage.

Morrow, V. (1999) 'Conceptualising social capital in relation to the well-being of children and young people: a critical review', *Sociological Review*, 47 (4): 744–65.

Morrow, V. (2000) '"Dirty looks" and "trampy places" in young people's accounts of community and neighbourhood: implications for health inequalities', *Critical Public Health*, 10: 141–52.

Moss, P. and Bennett, J. (2006) *Toward a New Pedagogical Meeting Place? Bringing Early Childhood into the Education System*, Briefing Paper for a Nuffield Educational Seminar, September.

Moss, P. and Petrie, P. (2002) *From Children's Services to Children's Spaces*. London: Taylor & Francis.

Moss, P., Dillon, J. and Statham, J. (2000) 'The "child in need" and "the rich child": discourses, constructions and practice', *Critical Social Policy*, 20 (2): 233.

Mouleart, F., Martinelli, F., Swyngedow, E. and Gonzales, S. (2005) 'Towards alternative model(s) of local innovation', *Urban Studies*, 42 (11): 1969–90.

Muldoon, S. (2004) *Is Symbolic Interactionism the Fifth Paradigm of*

Leadership?, School of Business Working Paper Series, Victoria University of Technology.

Mulgan, G. (2006) *The Process of Social Innovation*. Cambridge, MA: MIT Press.

Mulgan, G. with Tucker, S., Ali. R. and Sanders, B. (2007) *Social Innovation: What It Is, Why It Matters and How It Can Be Accelerated*, Skoll Centre for Social Entrepreneurship Working Paper, Oxford Saïd Business School.

Mullins, L. J. (2005) *Management and Organisational Behaviour*. London: Prentice Hall.

Mumford, M. D. (2002) 'Social innovation: ten cases from Benjamin Franklin', *Creativity Research Journal*, 14 (2): 253–66.

Mumford, M. D. and Gustafson, S. (1998) 'Creativity syndrome: integration, application and innovation', *Psychological Bulletin*, 103: 27–43.

Mumford, M. D. and Moertl, P. (2003) 'Cases of social innovation: lessons from two innovations in the 20th century', *Creativity Research Journal*, 15 (2): 261–6.

Munroe, E. (2011) *The Munro Review of Child Protection: Final Report: A Child-Centred System*. London: DoE.

Nakamura, J. and Shernoff, D. J. (2009) *Good Mentoring: Fostering Excellent Practice in Higher Education*. San Francisco: Jossey- Bass.

Northouse, P. G. (2007) *Leadership: Theory and Practice*, 4th edn. London: Sage.

O'Brien, M. and Penna, S. (1998) *Theorising Welfare*. London: Sage.

O'Neill, O. (2002) *A Question of Trust*, The BBC Reith Lectures. Cambridge: Cambridge University Press.

Oakland, J. S. (1993) *Total Quality Management*. Oxford: Butterworth-Heinemann.

Ochberg, R. L. (1994) 'Life stories and storied lives', in A. Lieblich and R. Josselson (eds), *Exploring Identity and Gender: The Narrative Study of Lives*. Thousand Oaks, CA: Sage, pp. 113–44.

OECD (2001a) *The Well-Being of Nations: The Role of Human and Social Capital*. Paris: OECD.

OECD (2001b) *Starting Strong I: Early Childhood Education and Care*. Paris: France.

Okely, J. (1975) 'The self and scientism', *Journal of the Anthropology Society of Oxford*, 6: 171–89.

Oliver, M. (1990) *The Politics of Disablement*. Basingstoke: Macmillan.

Ouchi, W. G. (1981) *Theory Z*. New York: Avon Books.

Ozga, J. (2000) 'New Labour, new teachers?', in J. Clarke, S. Gewirtz and E. McLaughlin (eds), *New Managerialism, New Welfare*. London: Sage.

Parsloe, E. (2009) *The Oxford School of Coaching and Mentoring in Mentor Set*. Online at: http://www.mentorset.org.uk/pages/mentoring.htm.

Parton, N. (2000) 'Some thoughts on the relationship between theory and practice in and for social work', *British Journal of Social Work*, 30: 449–63.

Pascarella, E. T. and Terenzini, P. T. (2005) *How College Affects Students: A Third Decade of Research*, Volume 2. San Francisco: Jossey-Bass.

Patrick, F., Forde, C. and McPhee, A. (2003) 'Challenging the "New Professionalism": from managerialism to pedagogy?', *Journal of In-Service Education*, 29 (2), 237–54.

Penna, S. and O'Brien, M. (1996) 'Postmodernism and social policy: a small step forwards?', *Journal of Social Policy*, 25 (1): 39–61.

Percy-Smith, B., Walsh, D. and Thompson, D. (2001) *Young, Homeless and Socially Excluded: Challenges for Policy and Practice*. Northampton: SOLAR Centre, University College Northampton/Children's Society.

Perri6, P., Leat, D., Seltzer, K. and Stoker, G. (2002) *Towards Holistic Governance: The New Reform Agenda*. Basingstoke: Palgrave.

Petri, H. L. (1996) *Motivation: Theory, Research, and Applications*, 4th edn. Pacific Grove, CA: Brooks/Cole.

Phillipson, M. (1972) 'Phenomenological philosophy and sociology', in P. Filmer (ed.), *New Directions in Socialogical Theory*. London: Collier Macmillan.

Piaget, J. (1975) *The Moral Judgement of the Child*. London: Routledge.

Pierson, C. (2004) *Beyond the Welfare State: The New Political Economy of Welfare*. Cambridge: Policy Press.

Piirto, J. (2004) *Understanding Creativity*. Scottsdale, AZ: Great Potential Press.

Pinkerton, J. (2000) 'Emerging agendas for family support', in J. Canavan, P. Dolan and J. Pinkerton (eds), *Family Support: Diversion from Diversity*. London: Jessica Kingsley.

Pinkerton, J. (2006) 'Reframing practice as family support: leaving care', in P. Dolan, J. Canavan and J. Pinkerton (eds), *Family Support as Reflective Practice*. London: Jessica Kingsley.

Pollitt, C. (1988) 'Bringing consumers into performance measurements: concepts, consequences and constraints', *Policy and Politics*, 16 (2): 77–87.

Porter, L. W., Steers, R. M., Mowday, R. T. and Boulian, P. V. (1974) 'Organizational commitment, job satisfaction, and turnover among psychiatric technicians', *Journal of Applied Psychology*, 59: 603–9.

Powell, M. and Hewitt, M. (2002) *Welfare State and Welfare Change*. Buckingham: Open University Press.

Power, S. (2001) '"Joined-up thinking": inter-agency partnerships in education action zones', in S. Riddell and L. Tett (eds), *Education, Social Justice and Inter-Agency Working: Joined Up or Fractured Policy?* London: Routledge.

Prout, A. (2000) 'Children's participation: control and self-realisation in British late modernity', *Children and Society*, 14: 304–16.

Prout, A. (2005) *The Future of Childhood*. London: FalmerRoutledge.

Prout, A., Symmonds, R. and Birchall, J. (2006) 'Reconnecting and extending the research agenda on children's participation: mutual incentives and the participation chain', in K. Tisdall, J. Davis, M. Hill and A. Prout (eds), *Children, Childhood and Social Inclusion*. London: Policy Press.

Pupavac, V. (2002) 'The international children's rights regime', in D. Chandler (ed.), *Rethinking Human Rights*. Basingstoke: Palgrave.

Rabinow, P. (1977) *Reflections on Fieldwork in Morocco*. Berkeley, CA: University of California Press.

Rice, R. (2007) *The Mentor's Use of Adult learning Theories: Are Theory and Practice Co-extensive?* Paper presented at BERA Annual Conference, Institute of Education, University of London, September.

Richards, R. (2007) 'Introduction', in R. Richards (ed.), *Everyday Creativity and New Views of Human Nature: Psychological, Social and Spiritual Perspectives*. Washington, DC: American Psychological Association.

Riddell, S. (2009) 'Social justice, equality and inclusion in Scottish education', *Discourse*, 30 (3): 283–97.

Riddell, S. and Tett, L. (eds) (2001) *Education, Social Justice and Inter-Agency Working: Joined Up or Fractured Policy?* London: Routledge.

Ritzer, G. (1992) *The McDonaldization of Society*. Thousand Oaks, CA: Pine Forge Press.

Rixon, A. (2008a) 'Working with change', in P. Foley and A. Rixon (eds), *Changing Children's Services: Working and Learning Together*. Bristol: Policy Press.

Rixon, A. (2008b) 'Positive practice relationships', in P. Foley and S. Leverett (eds), *Connecting with Children: Developing Working Relationships*. Bristol: Policy Press.

Roaf, C. (2002) *Coordinating Services for Included Children: Joined Up Action*. Buckingham: Open University Press.

Robinson, K. H. and Jones-Diaz, C. (2006) *Diversity and Difference in Early Childhood Education: Issues for Theory and Practice*. Maidenhead: Open University Press.

Rodd, J. (1994) *Leadership in Early Childhood*. Buckingham: Open University Press.

Rogers, C. and Freiberg, H. J. (1993) *Freedom to Learn*, 3rd edn. New York: Merrill.

Rogoff, B. (1993) 'Observing sociocultural activity on three planes', in J. V. Wertsch, P. del Río and A. Alvarez (eds), *Sociocultural Studies of Mind*. New York: Cambridge University Press, pp. 139–63.

Rorty, R. (1980) *Philosophy and the Mirror of Nature.* Princeton, NJ: Princeton University Press.

Rose, M. (1975) *Industrial Behaviour: Theoretical Developments Since Taylor.* London: Allen Lane.

Rossi, P., Lipsey, M. W. and Freeman, H. E. (2004) *Evaluation: A Systematic Approach,* 7th edn. Thousand Oaks, CA: Sage.

Rowe, A. (2005) 'The impact of Sure Start on health visiting', in J. Weinberger, C. Pickstone and P. Hannon (eds), *Learning from Sure Start: Working with Young Children and Their Families.* Maidenhead: Open University Press.

Rudge, C. (2010) 'Children's centres', in G. Pugh and B. Duffy (eds), *Contemporary Issues in the Early Years.* London: Sage.

Rugland, W. (1993) *Assuming the Mantle of Professionalism.* Valuation Actuary Symposium, USA.

Rushmer, R. and Pallis, G. (2002) 'Inter-professional working: the wisdom of integrated working and the disaster of blurred boundaries', *Public Money and Management,* October–December, pp. 59–66.

Salancik, G. R. and Pfeffer, J. (1977) 'An examination of need-satisfaction model of job attitudes', *Administrative Science Quarterly,* 22: 427–56.

Säljö, R. (2003) 'Epilogue: from transfer to boundary-crossing', in T. Tuomi-Gröhn and Y. Engeström (eds), *Between School and Work: New Perspectives on Transfer and Boundary-Crossing.* London: Elsevier.

Scardamalia, M. and Bereiter, C. (2006) *FCL and Knowledge Building: A Continuing Dialogue.* Institute for Knowledge Innovation and Technology, University of Toronto.

Schein, E. H. (1999) *Organizational Learning: What Is New?* Cambridge, MA: Society for Organisational Learning.

Schienstock, G. and Hämäläinen, T. (2001) *Transformation of the Finnish Innovation System: A Network Approach,* SITRA Reports Series 7. Helsinki: Hakapaino OY.

Schlundt, D. G. and McFall, R. M. (1985) 'New directions in the assessment of social skills', in M. A. Milan and L. L'Abate (eds), *Handbook of Social Skills Training and Research.* New York: Wiley, pp. 231–49.

Schön, D. (1987) *Educating the Reflective Practitioner.* San Francisco: Jossey-Bass.

Schumpeter, J. (1934) *The Theory of Economic Development.* Cambridge, MA: Harvard University Press.

Schwandt, T. (1996) 'Farewell to criteriology', *Qualitative Inquiry,* 2 (1): 58–72.

Scott, F. (2006) *The Representation of Integration in Guidance and*

Documents Relating to Children's Services Plans. MSc Childhood Studies dissertation, Edinburgh University.

Scottish Credit and Qualifications Framework and Scottish Social Services Council (2007) *Recognition of Prior Informal Learning: Guidance and Resources for Mentors and Learners*. Dundee: SSSC.

Scottish Executive (2004) *The Sum of Its Parts: The Development of Integrated Community Schools in Scotland*. Edinburgh: HMSO.

Scottish Executive (2005a) *21st Century Review of Social Work: Leadership and Management Sub Group Report*. Edinburgh: HMSO.

Scottish Executive (2005b) *Getting It Right for Every Child in Scotland: Consultation on the Review of the Children's Hearing System*. Edinburgh: HMSO.

Scottish Government (2001) *For Scotland's Children Report*. Edinburgh: HMSO.

Scottish Government (2004) *Additional Support for Learning (Scotland) Act 2004*. Edinburgh: HMSO.

Scottish Government (2007) *New Scottish Government and Getting It Right for Every Child Update*. Edinburgh: HMSO.

Scottish Government (2010) *National Guidance for Child Protection in Scotland 2010*. Edinburgh: Edinburgh.

Scottish Home and Health Department (1964) *Kilbrandon Report*. Edinburgh: HMSO.

Scottish Office (1995) *The Children (Scotland) Act 1995: Regulation and Guidance*. Edinburgh: HMSO.

Searle, J. R. (1980) 'Minds, brains, and programs', *Behavioral and Brain Sciences*, 3 (3): 417–57.

Searle, J. and Soler, M. (2004) *Language and Social Sciences. Dialogue Between John Searle and CREA*. Barcelona: El Roure.

Seddon, J. (2003) *Freedom from Command and Control: A Better Way to Make the Work Work*. Buckingham: Vanguard Education.

Seddon, J. (2008) *Systems Thinking in the Public Sector: The Failure of the Reform Regime – A Manifesto for a Better Way*. Axminster: Triarchy Press.

Senge, P. M. (1990) *The Fifth Discipline: The Art and Practice of the Learning Organization*. New York: Doubleday.

Sepúlveda, G. (2001) *What Is Expansive Learning?* Temuco, Chile: Department of Education, Universidad de La Frontera.

Shain, F. and Gleeson, D. (1999) 'Under new management: changing conceptions of teacher professionalism and policy in the further education sector', *Journal of Education Policy*, 14 (4): 445–62.

Shapiro, E. C. (1996) *Fad Surfing in the Boardroom*. Oxford: Capstone.

Sheldon, B. (2001) 'The validity of evidence-based practice in social work: a reply to Stephen Webb', *British Journal of Social Work*, 31: 801–9.

Shiba, S. (1998) 'Leadership and breakthrough', *Centre for Quality of Management Journal*, 7 (2): 10–22.

Shier, H. (2001) 'Pathways to participation: openings, opportunities and obligations: a new model for enhancing children's participation in decision-making, in line with article 12.1 of the United Nations Convention on the Rights of the Child', *Children and Society*, 15 (2): 107–17.

Shore, C. and Wright, S. (2000) 'Coercive accountability: the rise of the audit culture in higher education', in M. Strathern (ed.), *Audit Cultures: Anthropological Studies in Accountability and the Academy*. London: Routledge.

Simmons, L. (2007) *Social Care Governance: A Practice Workbook*. London: Social Care Institute for Excellence.

Sims, D., Fineman, S. and Gabriel, Y. (1993) *Organising and Organisations: An Introduction*. London: Sage.

Sinclair, R. and Franklin, A. (2000) *A Quality Protects Briefing: Young People's Participation*. London: Department of Health.

SITRA (2005) *Making Finland a Leading Country in Innovation: Innovation Programme*. Helsinki: SITRA.

Skye, E., Meddings, S. and Dimmock, B. (2003) 'Theories for understanding people', in J. Henderson and D. Atkinson (eds), *Managing Care in Context*. London: Routledge.

Smith, A. B., Grima, G., Gaffney, M. and Powell, K. (2000) *Early Childhood Education: Literature Review Report to the Ministry of Education*. Dunedin, New Zealand: University of Otago, Children's Issues Centre.

Smith, M. (2009) *What Is Family Support Work? A Case Study Within the Context of One Local Authority in Scotland*. EdD, University of Edinburgh.

Smith, M. and Davis, J. M. (2010) 'Constructions of family support: lessons from the field', *Administration Journal of the Institute of Public Administration: Ireland*, 58: 69–83.

Smith, M. and Whyte, B. (2007) 'Social education and social pedagogy: reclaiming a Scottish tradition in social work', *European Journal of Social Work*, 11 (1): 15–28.

Spinosa, C., Flores, F. and Dreyfus, H. L. (1997) *Disclosing New Worlds: Entrepreneurship, Democratic Action and Cultivation of Solidarity*. Cambridge, MA: MIT Press.

Stalker, K. and McArthur, K. (2010) 'Child abuse, child protection and disabled children: a review of recent research', *Child Abuse Review*, online.

Sternberg, D. H., Feldman, J. and Nakamura, M. (2004) *Creativity: From Potential to Realization*. Washington, DC: American Psychological Association.

Sternberg, R. J. (2003) *Wisdom, Intelligence, and Creativity Synthesized.* Cambridge: Cambridge University Press.

Sternberg, R. J. (2007) *Wisdom, Intelligence, and Creativity Synthesized.* Cambridge: Cambridge University Press.

Stevenson, O. (1998) *Neglected Children: Issues and Dilemmas.* Oxford: Blackwell Science.

Stewart, C. and Cash, W. (2000) *Interviewing: Principle and Practice.* Boston, MA: McGraw-Hill.

Stone, B. and Rixon, A. (2008) 'Towards integrated working', in P. Foley and A. Rixon (eds), *Changing Children's Services: Working and Learning Together.* Bristol: Policy Press.

Stradling, B., MacNeil, M. and Berry, H. (2009) *Changing Professional Practice and Culture to Get It Right for Every Child.* Edinburgh: Scottish Government.

Taket, A. R. and White, L. A. (2000) *Partnership and Participation: Decision-Making in the Multiagency Setting.* Chichester: John Wiley.

Taylor, F. W. (1964) *Scientific Management – Comprising Shop Management, the Principles of Scientific Management and Testimony before the Special House Committee.* New York: Harper & Row.

Thomas, N. (2007) 'Towards a theory of children's participation', *International Journal of Children's Rights*, 15 (2): 199–218.

Thomas, N. (2009) 'Conclusion: autonomy, dialogue and recognition', in N. Thomas (ed.), *Children, Politics and Communication: Participation at the Margins.* Bristol: Policy Press.

Tisdall, E. K. M. (1995) *The Children (Scotland) Act 1995: Developing Policy and Law for Scotland's Children.* Edinburgh: TSO.

Tisdall, E. K. M. and Davis, J. (2004) 'Making a difference? Bringing children's and young people's views into policy-making', *Children and Society*, 18 (2): 77–96.

Tisdall, E. K., Wallace, J. and Bell, A. (2006) *Seamless Services: Smoother Lives: Assessing the Impact of Local Preventative Services on Children and Their Families.* Edinburgh: Children in Scotland.

Tisdall, K., Davis, J. M. and Gallagher, M. J. (eds) (2009) *Research with Children and Young People.* London: Sage.

Tomlinson, K. (2003) *Effective Inter-Agency Working: A Review of the Literature and Examples from Practice.* Slough: NFER.

Trist, E. L. and Bamforth, K. W. (1951) 'Some social and psychological consequences of the longwall method of coal-getting', *Human Relations*, 4 (3): 38.

Tsoukas, H. (1993) 'The road to emancipation is through organizational development: a critical evaluation of total systems intervention', *Systems Practice*, 6 (1): 53–70.

Tuomi, I. (2002) *Networks of Innovation: Change and Meaning in the Age of the Internet.* Oxford: Oxford University Press.

Tuomi-Gröhn, T. (2003) 'Developmental transfer as goal of internship in practical nursing', in T. Tuomi-Gröhn and Y. Engeström (eds), *Between School and Work: New Perspectives on Transfer and Boundary-Crossing*. London: Elsevier.

Turkie, A. (2010) 'More than crumbs from the table: a critique of youth parliaments as models of representation for marginalised young people', in B. Percy-Smith and N. Thomas (eds), *A Handbook of Children and Young People's Participation: Perspectives from Theory and Practice*. London: Routledge.

Turnbull, A. (2009) *Using Line Management*. Melbourne: School of Education.

UEA (2007) *National Evaluation of the Children's Trust: Children's Trust Pathfinders*. Norwich: University of East Anglia.

Unsworth, K. (2001) 'Unpacking creativity', *Academy of Management Review*, 26 (2): 289–97.

UPIAS (Union of the Physically Impaired Against Segregation)/ Disability Alliance (1976) *Fundamental Principles of Disability*. London: Methuen.

Urwick, L. (1952) *Notes on the Theory of Organisation*. New York: American Management Association.

Van de Ven, A. H. (1986) 'Central problems in the management of innovation', *Management Science*, 32 (5): 590–607.

Vincent, C. (2003) 'Introduction', in C. Vincent (ed.), *Social Justice, Education and Identity*. London: Routledge.

Visser, M. (2007) 'Deutero-learning in organizations: a review and a reformulation', *Academy of Management Review*, 32 (2): 659–67.

Von Hippel, E. (2005) *Democratizing Innovation*. Cambridge, MA: MIT Press.

Vygotsky, L. S. (1995) *Problemy defectologii* [*Problems of Defectology*]. Moscow: Prosvecshenie Press.

Waldrop, M. M. (1992) *Complexity: The Emerging Science at the Edge of Order and Chaos*. New York: Simon & Schuster.

Walker, G. (2004) 'The evolution of coaching: patterns, icons and freedom', *International Journal of Evidence-Based Coaching and Mentoring*, 2 (2): 16–41.

Walker, G. (2008) *Working Together for Children: A Critical Introduction to Multi-Agency Working*. London: Continuum.

Walshe, K. and Shortell, S. M. (2004) 'Social regulation of healthcare organizations in the United States: developing a framework for evaluation', *Health Services Management Research*, 17: 79–99.

Walter, I., Nutley, S., Percy-Smith, J., McNeish, D. and Frost, S. (2004) *Improving the Use of Research in Social Care Practice*. London: Social Care Institute for Excellence.

Watson, D. (2003) 'Defining quality care for looked after children:

frontline workers' perspectives on standards and all that?', *Child and Family Social Work*, 8: 67–77.

Wax, R. H. (1971) *Doing Fieldwork: Warnings and Advice*. Chicago: University of Chicago Press.

Webb, R. and Vulliamy, G. (2001) 'Joining up solutions: the rhetoric and practice of inter-agency cooperation', *Children and Society*, 15: 315–22.

Weber, M. (1947) *The Theory of Social and Economic Organization*. New York: Oxford University Press.

Webster, S. (2000) *Study of the Impact of Organisational Re-Structuring in the Children's Society*. London: TCS.

Weick, K. E., Sutcliffe, K. M. and Obstfeld, D. (2005) 'Organizing and the process of sensemaking', *Organization Science*, 16 (4): 409–21.

Weinstein, J. (1994) *Sewing the Seams for a Seamless Service: A Review of Developments in Interprofessional Education and Training*. London: CCETSW.

Wells, G. (2001) *Action, Talk, and Text: Learning and Teaching Through Inquiry*, Practitioner Inquiry Series. Williston, VT: Teachers College Press.

Welsh Assembly Government (2004) *Rights to Action*. Cardiff: WAG.

Welsh Assembly Government (2008) *We Are On the Way: A Policy Agenda to Transform the Lives of Disabled Children*. Cardiff: WAG.

West, M. A. (2002) 'Sparkling fountains or stagnant ponds? An integrative model of creativity and innovation implementation within groups', *Applied Psychology: An International Review*, 51 (3): 355–86.

Wilding, P. (1994) 'Maintaining quality in human services', *Social Policy and Administration*, 28 (1): 49–72.

Wilson, V. and Pirrie, A. (2000) *Multi-Disciplinary Team Working: Indicators of Good Practice*. Edinburgh: SCRE.

Winton, P., McCollum, J. A. and Catlet, C. (1997) *Reforming Personnel Preparation in Early Intervention*. Baltimore, MD: Paul H. Brookes.

Wolvin, A. and Coakley, C. (1993) *Perspectives on Listening*. Norwood, NJ: Ablex.

Woodhead, M. (2009) 'Child development and the development of childhood', in J. Qvortrup et al. (eds), *Handbook of Childhood Studies*. London: Palgrave.

Woodman, R. W., Sawyer, J. E. and Griffin, R. W. (1993) 'Toward a theory of organizational creativity', *Academy of Management Review*, 18: 293–321.

Young, I. M. (1990) *Justice and the Politics of Difference*. Princeton, NJ: Princeton University Press.

Index

Added to a page number 't' denotes a table.